Four Th

Four Thousand Days

My Journey From Prison To Business Success

Duane Jackson

First published in 2015

Copyright © Duane Jackson 2015

The right of Duane Jackson to be identified as the Author
of the Work has been asserted by him in accordance
with the Copyright, Designs and Patents Act 1988

ISBN-13: 978-1511431927
ISBN-10: 151143192X

Published by
CreateSpace Independent Publishing Platform

Thanks

To those who helped me in the process of putting this book together: Patrick Johnson, Barbara Benton, Steve O'Hear and Richard Newton

To the awesome people I've worked with over the years who don't get a mention – none of this would have been possible without you.

To everyone who works for or supports The Prince's Trust and the amazing work they do.

And most importantly, for her infinite patience and faith: Nadia Jackson

"If you don't design your own life plan, chances are you'll fall into someone else's plan. And guess what they have planned for you? Not much."

- Jim Rohn

CONTENTS

Foreword from The Rt Hon Lord Young of Graffham

FOREWORD

When I first met Duane I was quite taken with his business. This was long before The Cloud was thought of and the idea of keeping the program on your own server and leasing access to it to your customers was so remarkable that I quite overlooked the fact that his customers were barely into double figures. I made the mistake that most of us who invest in technology companies make. We look at the idea, at the technology used and overlook the person behind it.

I knew that Duane had been in jail, had been sentenced for something that I was told was drugs related and I also knew that the Prince's Trust had recently given him his chance. I had been part of the Prince's Trust for many years and that was how we met. In time I became his Mentor and the rest is in this book. What I did not appreciate at the time, and only realised as the years went by, was how quite remarkable, and unfortunately how unusual, his journey had been.

At the beginning I was helping him as part of my work for the Prince's Trust. As the months and then the years went by I began to realise that here was a young man of ability with drive and determination, who had had little chance, up to then, to show what he was made of. As the business grew, his self-confidence grew with it and as his confidence grew, so did his abilities. How, I began to wonder, could someone with little or no formal education achieve what he was in the process of achieving. Eventually I realised his achievements were in spite of his education and not because of it. How many, I wondered, had switched off during their early years at school, and when they left, at the first opportunity, had little to show for it. Even more, how many had let their lack of success in school convince themselves that they were failures?

A few years later I was back in government and as part of my responsibilities created Start-Up Loans, which gave an opportunity, for anyone who wanted to work for themselves, to have a loan of £5,000 and a Mentor. Many hundreds are doing so week after week. This time

I remembered Duane and we have introduced a scheme that will enable people still in jail to create their business plan and then start their business as soon as they leave, of course with the continuing help of a Mentor. It is still early days, but I hope that in time we will create many more Duanes, who, even if they are not as successful as he has been, will be able to support themselves and their family and regain their full place in society.

One of the unexpected results is that I have gained even more than Duane from our association. I had all the fun and excitement of being involved with a successful start-up (although, happily, little of the hard work), the continuing excitement as the business grew and of course the successful conclusion with the sale of the business. I think I enjoyed my time with Duane and KashFlow more than I had any time with any of my own businesses. Then I also began to realise that my own conventional upbringing had been a very sheltered one and that there were very many in society had not been so fortunate, people with skills and ability that have been denied even the modest start in life that I had enjoyed.

Although I had been long concerned with young people who obtained little or no benefit from their school years, going back to the days of the Youth Training Scheme in the early eighties, I had not considered the innate ability of many who have fallen by the wayside. I hope that a result of the work I did then and I shall be doing over the next few years in education, we shall see that many, who even if they do make a mistake, will be given an opportunity to recover.

This is a story which should give heart to many.

David Young
Graffham, April 2015

Chapter One

MY NIGHT WITH THE DEA

The flight from London to Atlanta was was pretty uneventful. I was glad of the chance to get some sleep after a heavy night drinking.

My hand luggage was stuffed with drugs and as I got to the top of the escalator, I spotted two sniffer dogs. My heart skipped a beat. I couldn't turn back. I could only stand in the crowd on the escalator slowly descending. It took forever. I could see them getting closer and closer. Every passing second seemed to add weight to my bag. I had no idea if Ecstasy had a smell that could be detected by dogs. It's not something I had even thought about. I was trying to keep calm and not look nervous, even as my stomach was tying itself in knots. I became paranoid that one of the dogs was staring at me. My palms were sweating and I felt nauseous. I stepped off the escalator and waited for the dogs to pounce. They didn't.

A wave of relief came over me. I'd never taken Ecstasy myself but if I could have bottled the feeling I had just endured I am sure I could have sold it and made a fortune. Thank fuck this was to be my last trip, I never wanted to go through that experience again. I just needed to collect my checked-in suitcase, complete the deal and be on my way to see Simone. I couldn't wait to tell her about what just happened. I laughed to myself about how scared I was.

'Excuse me sir, do you have all of your luggage?' asked a man in uniform who had just materialised in front of me.

'No. I'm still waiting,' I replied.

He smiled, nodded and walked away.

Ahead of me I could see lots of Customs officers busy checking cases. At Gatwick, Heathrow or JFK I had never seen all of the Customs tables in use. But here it was like a jumble sale - every table had an open suitcase on it with a uniformed officer searching.

My bag appeared and I headed straight for the *Nothing to Declare* lane. My mind was telling my legs to move faster and my legs were shouting back to slow down, don't attract attention! That initial relief disappeared and I began to panic again.

'Step this way please,' an officer ordered. FUCK!

He took my suitcase and gave it a thorough going over. It was clean, of course.

But my shoulder bag … would they notice it?

Pathetically, I tried to push it further round my back, willing it to disappear.

'And that one,' he demanded, indicating the bag that refused to disappear between my shoulder blades. Now I knew the game was up.

He pulled out the talcum powder, took off the lid and emptied it onto the stainless steel counter. I saw clouds of talcum powder, followed by dozens and dozens of tubes of Ecstasy tablets, all wrapped in cling film. Not a word was uttered but I could tell the officer was pleased with himself. How? Because the bastard started humming a merry tune as he worked through the rest of the bag.

Then he started to take the back off the speaker. There were thousands of pills there. He had hit the jackpot.

'Are these yours?' The guy who had previously looked bored silly and as if he'd have rather been at home - doing whatever it was Customs officers do on their day off - was somehow replaced by his identical twin brother, full of smiles and the joys of life.

'Yes' I stammered. He asked me what they were. 'Ecstasy tablets' I admitted.

More officers swarmed on me. I was taken to a holding cell, a large windowless room close to the Customs area. I realised that after the emotional roller coaster of the last few minutes, I was remarkably calm. I guess I was resigned to whatever was to happen now was out of my hands and I just needed to go with the flow. I realised I was probably going to be a bit late getting to New York. Naively, I thought there was probably going to be a mountain of paperwork to get through before they gave me a formal slap on the wrist and sent me on my way with a cheery 'Have a nice day!' At worst, they wouldn't let me into the country and instead send me packing back to London without even seeing Simone.

Hang on... London. Allen was staying at my flat while I was away. He'd be wondering why I hadn't called to let him know I'd cleared Customs. By now he would have started to worry that something had gone wrong.

Alone, I was in that holding cell for what felt like hours, with my head spinning from the millions of thoughts racing through my brain. At some point I managed to stop kidding myself that I was going to be free any time soon. This was Georgia, they took this kind of thing pretty damn seriously here, didn't they?

For the first time it hit home just how much trouble I could be in. I hadn't set out on the path of a career criminal. I wasn't a hardened East End thug. I had just fallen into an opportunity to earn an extra bit of money to pay my bills and keep the roof over my head.

Eventually, the door opened and two guys I hadn't seen before walked in.

Special Agent Shelby introduced himself and his partner, Anton, both from the Drug Enforcement Administration, the DEA. I'd heard of them, they were the stuff of Hollywood movies. Anton was black, stocky and in his late thirties. Shelby was white, tall and skinny with long hair. He looked like a drug user, certainly not a cop or a DEA agent. Maybe he was also an undercover drugs officer. I couldn't place his age. Maybe a young 40 or an old-looking 25.

They both wore plain clothes, jeans and T-shirts, but with their badges hanging from their trousers and packing guns in their holsters. Shelby suddenly started scaring me witless by saying I was looking at 25 years in jail and a $1 million fine. I thought he was winding me up. But he wasn't joking, that's exactly what I was facing.

They started quizzing me about the drugs. Where did I get them? And, more importantly, who was meeting me in Atlanta? I avoided answering as best I could and tried to plead ignorance. If anyone ever really does meet a stranger in a pub and is asked to carry drugs for them, then good bloody luck getting anyone to believe you.

I was playing dumb in a desperate bid to buy time. I knew by now that Allen would have known that it had all gone wrong. With no coded phone call from me to confirm I had cleared Customs, the whole State side operation would have been alerted too.

Shelby had finally had enough and gave me an ultimatum: Help them lay a trap for the American buyers or go straight to jail.

'Do not pass Go? Do not collect two hundred pounds?' I asked with a smile. I was actually starting to enjoy myself. It all felt a bit surreal.

'Dollars,' said Anton. 'You're in my country now'. He wasn't smiling.

Great line, I thought. "You're in *my* country now". I could imagine Harrison Ford saying that to the Russian baddie.

I couldn't grass up my friends, it just wasn't an option. I certainly wasn't going to give up the Americans either. It was inevitable that I was going to go to prison at some point. My goal now was to delay that for as long as possible, even if just for a couple more hours.

I did my best to look thoughtful, as if I was mentally struggling with a big difficult decision. 'OK' I said. 'I'll help you catch the buyers.' I thought I could string out their questioning and play along with the game. The buyers would be long gone as I hadn't made the call to London to say I was past Customs.

'If you hadn't got stopped, what would you have done once you got out of the airport?' asked Shelby. 'Here's a clue: the answer isn't "I don't know".'

'I would have gone to a hotel and waited for a phone call' I lied.

'Which hotel?'

When I'd been searched at Customs, I'd had a scrap of paper in my pocket. On one side was Simone's name and phone number. On the other side it read 'Holiday Inn Crowne Plaza' and an Atlanta phone number - the results of my last-minute rushed research that morning before leaving home.

'Which hotel?' he asked again, getting impatient. He pulled out a folded up polythene packet from his back pocket. It had my scrap of paper in it. He put it on the table in front of me 'This hotel?'

I just nodded.

'So this is the hotel.' Anton said. It wasn't a question. It was a statement. And it was aimed at Shelby, not at me.

They smiled at each other, extremely pleased with themselves and their well-honed interrogation techniques. The pair had a major drugs bust in their sights. Their enthusiasm was bordering on cockiness.

'So what are we waiting for? Let's get you checked in' Anton declared, before they both left the room. He was certainly smiling now.

Ten minutes later they were back but confused and not pleased with me. They realised the Holiday Inn and Crowne Plaza were two different hotels, not the name of one.

I resisted the urge to say 'Well, duh!' Surely this should have been self-evident to two highly-trained drug enforcement officers who were on their own patch. Had it really taken them so long to figure out?

I continued playing dumb and just said, 'Are they? I didn't realise'.

'Which one would you have gone to?'

I wasn't sure. Maybe Crowne Plaza as I had written it first. Shelby and Anton couldn't fathom out the conundrum and called for their superior.

The Boss Man arrived. I never got to know his name. He was older, in his mid-fifties perhaps and, although smartly dressed, I couldn't help thinking he was wearing a cheap suit for a man calling the shots.

He looked me up and and down as he entered the cell and was obviously underwhelmed.

'Is this the guy?' he asked Anton in the thickest southern drawl I'd ever heard.

He wanted to hear my whole story for himself. I found it difficult to understand his accent and I kept asking him to repeat himself. At the same time he was baffled by my East London accent. It was quite comical: here we were talking the same language but neither could make head nor tail of what the other was saying.

Anton began to interpret. Boss Man asked if they called me Steady Eddie back in London.

I frowned. 'What do you mean?'

'Wod yummin?' said Boss Man, obviously not understanding me.

Anton translated for me and the big man explained that someone in as much trouble as me seemed incredibly calm. I just laughed, which was probably not the best reaction.

The truth is that it didn't feel real. It was as if it was happening to someone else. I was struggling to take these guys seriously. And the American accents just added to the feeling that I was trapped in a film.

Finally, someone decided for no apparent reason I would have definitely gone to the Crowne Plaza and not the Holiday Inn. With that they booked me in over the phone and within minutes we were suddenly on the move. For the first time in hours I left the airport and I realised it was now quite late, probably about 11pm.

Shelby and Anton, with four other officers, escorted me through a maze of corridors in the airport and we left the building through a nondescript side exit. I was shoved into the back of a big Jeep with blacked-out windows, squeezed in between two burly agents in the back. Anton and Shelby were in the front.

As the car-cum-tank moved out of the airport, Shelby put on some music and kept turning around and smiling at me. It dawned on me that he was expecting a reaction to the music, so I listened a bit closer.

'*Bad boys, bad boys. What you gonna do? What you gonna do when they come for you?*' I vaguely knew the song but had no idea what Shelby wanted. He stopped the CD and enthusiastically explained that it was the theme tune from the show *Cops* and he always played it when he made an arrest.

'I've never seen it' I confessed.

Shelby was clearly disappointed and we drove the rest of the way in silence.

It didn't take long before we came to a stop at a petrol station. On one side was the Holiday Inn. On the other side, not quite as tall, the Crowne Plaza. Shelby got out immediately and disappeared in the general direction of the latter.

'Right. Let's get this show on the road' boomed Anton, pointing at the hotel.

'Go up to reception and give your name' he ordered. 'You're booked into Room 709. You'll see agents you probably recognise from the airport. Don't make any attempt at eye contact and don't talk to them'.

'As you walk from here to the hotel there are 10 guns pointed at you, so don't even think about trying anything stupid.'

Too late, I thought. I already have.

I wasn't planning on doing anything. I didn't know what they thought I could do. Maybe summon a helicopter to rescue me? They must have been watching too much James Bond.

'Quiet on set,' I muttered to myself as I stepped out of the car and made the short walk to the hotel. It felt weird to be out in the fresh evening air on my own. It was certainly refreshing after the crowded cell and car but short-lived as I very quickly reached the foyer.

Without difficulty, I spotted the agents, including Shelby. I walked straight past him and as I did I sensed him walk into my shadow and follow me as I approached reception. He was right on my shoulder as I walked up to the desk. Yeah, Shelby, that seems really natural, mate.

'My name is Jackson and I have a reservation' I told the pretty receptionist

'Certainly sir' she replied, tapping into her keyboard.

'No reservation here for you.' as she looked up from the screen. 'But we have vacancies - how many nights will you be staying with us?'

'Sorry, but I do have a reservation. It's for room 709.'

'You can't have, sir – we don't even have a seventh floor' she explained.

The next 30 seconds seemed to go on forever. I was just standing there looking at her. The receptionist must have thought I was crazy. I didn't know what to do or say. I was standing like a statue, feet set in concrete and staring blankly at her. I could feel Shelbys presence next to me but was desperate not to turn and make eye contact with him. I didn't want to piss off the DEA.

Shelby finally leaned over, discreetly showed her his badge and confirmed we had booked Room 709. She struggled to maintain her patience and her smile had been replaced by a look of frustration. She repeated to him that they didn't have a Room 709. Pulling out his notebook, Shelby gave her a reservation number.

'Ah!' the receptionist brightened up. 'I see the problem! That's a reservation code for the Holiday Inn just across the way there.'

I was still standing there like a complete idiot, staring at some fixed point in the distance, as if someone had removed my batteries. But I could feel the energy seeping out of Shelby.

He babbled into his radio. Instantly a load of guys who had been sitting around reading newspapers in the hotel lobby, stood up simultaneously and walked towards the front of the building.

'Come with me' Shelby demanded, grabbing my arm and whispering 'Walk with me out of the lobby.' Outside, the undercover agents were standing together.

They had obviously given up on the whole discretion thing as at least two of them had put on their DEA baseball caps, while one had the logo on the back of his jacket. They looked a formidable sight. Any would-be drug buyers in the area, especially my imaginary ones, would certainly have been scared off by now.

Boss Man was there, not looking happy. Shelby still hadn't let go of my arm and I thought he'd forgotten he still had hold of me. So I got to listen to the entire conversation that followed. It turned out that the phone number on my scrap of paper was for the Holiday Inn. So, despite being told to book me in to the Crowne Plaza, some underling didn't check the correct number and simply called what I had written

d   o   w   n   .

Given the huge DEA presence and the fact that it was hours after I should have checked in to the hotel to wait for this supposed phone call, it'd be fair to assume my buyers would have given up by now.

Well, you'd be wrong. The evening's entertainment was only just getting started. Unbelievably, Boss Man decided it was worth going across the road to the Holiday Inn for *Drugs Bust: Take Two.*

The big car pulled up and I was chucked into it, flanked by my new friends. We went through the charade of driving back to the garage, the only difference being I was told to go directly to my room on the seventh floor and nowhere near the reception desk. By the time I reached Room 709, its door and that of the adjoining room were wide open and everywhere was swarming with agents.

There was a buzz of excitement in the air but I could only feel sorry for them as there were no drug dealers about to call to arrange a big pick-up. I was like a bad Santa, leaving them with no presents to unwrap.

At first I was told to sit on the bed and not move. The room next door was being set up as a monitoring station and I watched the agents as they discussed where to position their cameras and microphones. They even went to the extent of hiding a camera on top of the curtain rail and bugging the phone. It was all very elaborate.

'Where will they sit?' I suddenly realised I was being quizzed.

'Sorry?' I asked.

'Where will they sit? Your buyers, where will they sit?' said yet another agent, one I'd not previously seen.

Where would a non-existent drug dealer sit when doing a non-existent drug deal? I wondered.

'On the chair?' I replied without a hint of facetiousness.

'Right, the chair!' he said, as if he'd just had a eureka moment, remembering the well-known fact that drug dealers simply loved a good sit down in a chair. Time to move the room's only chair from its natural place in the corner to an odd angle near the foot of the bed. He disappeared next door, returning again to adjust the position of the chair slightly to get a clearer shot from his curtain-cam.

'Doesn't that look a bit silly there?' I asked.

Boss Man agreed with me and ordered it back where it was.

'But it's out of shot there,' protested Agent Curtain Cam.

'Then move the damn camera!' said the head honcho, beginning to lose patience.

The chair went back to its original position and the camera was installed inside a plastic bin. This was going to be interesting I thought, genuinely curious to see how he was going to disguise the hole he'd made in the side of the bin for the camera. He pulled the bin bag down to just above the hole. It was not as inconspicuous as it was on the curtain rail but it'd probably do.

But then, rather than put the bin back on the floor, he carefully positioned it on the side unit next to the TV. Not only did it look stupidly out of place but given its new altitude you could now quite clearly see the hole for the camera. He checked the monitor in the other room and was apparently happy with the view.

The boss walked in and looked at it. 'Uh oh.' I thought he was going to kick off but either he'd given up on getting any decent work out of his men or that's where he was used to seeing bins, he seemed perfectly happy with the set up.

I was thankful I was not really planning to do a deal in this room. Anyone who came into that room would have taken one look at the bin-with-a-hole-pointing-at-the-chair and walked straight back out again, potentially shooting me as they left.

Eventually, calmness descended over the room. The cameras were all installed and tested time and time again. Shelby, Anton, a couple of other agents and Boss Man were with me, just chilling, but excitedly waiting for the call ... the call that was never going to happen. Agent Bin Cam must have been on monitoring duty next door because he was not with us. I wondered how long they would wait?

We had not eaten for hours and hunger was starting to set in. An agent was dispatched to McDonald's and I ordered six chicken nuggets, chips, barbecue sauce and a Coca-Cola. As we tucked in, small talk turned to England and we sat chatting like a group of pals about television programmes and other trivia.

Every now and then the boss would chip in with a 'what did he say?'

and Anton would do his Anglo-American translation. But as we continued to talk I noticed a change in the chief's mood as he began to tire at the lack of any real action. He still couldn't understand my accent and was beginning to get the right hump. I could only imagine that the penny was beginning to drop and the phone call was just not going to happen.

Then his mood blackened completely and he started shouting, accusing me of lying and wasting their time. Well, he wasn't wrong there. The louder he became the less and less I could understand what he was saying. Anton had to interpret for me and that made him madder still. He had finally lost it. The game was up.

What happened next could only be described as a minor miracle. The phone rang. How could this be happening? Who on this planet could be phoning me? There was not another living soul (apart from my new DEA pals) who knew I was in Room 709. But whoever was on the other end of that phone certainly caused a commotion. To be more precise, all hell broke loose.

Boss Man quietened everyone down and told me to answer the phone. No translation required.

I picked up the receiver and as soon as I said 'hello', the shrill sound of an agent's radio filled the room. Some dickhead had forgotten to turn his radio off!

The phone went dead, most likely because the caller heard my British accent and realised they had the wrong room or maybe they weren't expecting a male voice and didn't have the courtesy to apologise. But Boss Man was convinced the radio had scared off my contact. The guilty agent had the bollocking of his life. I was just grateful that he was shouting at someone else.

They convinced themselves the buyer was going to call again but I knew differently. He wouldn't because he didn't exist. Everything I'd told them was a fiction.

We sat twiddling our thumbs for another hour or so. Boss Man realised he'd got me wrong and I wasn't a lying time-waster after all, but tempers were once again becoming frayed and I realised that the hapless agent was nowhere to be seen. He was probably on the first plane to Alaska for a new posting.

The boss must have been totting up all the overtime being racked up by his agents for all this effort, which was so far hopelessly unrewarded. He was bombarding me with questions but I could only play dumb. I just kept repeating that I was instructed to go to the hotel and wait for the call.

He suddenly remembered about the name Simone and the New York phone number on the piece of paper.

'Tell me about her again' he demanded.

I saw no reason to lie about Simone. I was relieved we were on a topic that I was happy to talk about without being evasive. I'd briefly explained who she was earlier in the night but now I spoke enthusiastically about her being my girlfriend and studying drama at university in New York. I told them I was going to buy a domestic ticket to go to see her once the deal was done. For once I was not telling porkies. But he became obsessed with the idea that she was part of the deal and the destination for the drugs. I just laughed. There was only way to find out, he insisted: 'Phone her now.'

It was the middle of the night in New York, too, but he didn't give a damn, demanding I called Simone to tell her I had been delayed. I didn't really have an option. I had to make that call. And they were listening in. No-one needed to be told to make sure their radio was off this time.

Simone was genuinely surprised to hear my voice. I explained I'd been held up and could not get to New York till the next morning. She said it was fine and I suspect she probably wanted to get back to sleep. But Boss Man moved his finger in a circular motion to indicate I should keep the conversation going. I was struggling to think what to say but remembered the play she was excited for us to see together, so I asked if she had managed to get tickets for *Snakebite*.

'Yes, yes. I have two tickets for us' she said, 'but I haven't been able to get an extra one for Natalie. She really wanted to come with us.'

I had been concentrating on talking to Simone. So when I looked back up at the agents in the room I was amazed to see the change in their demeanor. They were all smiles! Boss Man was running his finger across his neck indicating that I should end the call. We should have done sign language from the outset! I said goodnight to Simone and put down the phone, fully aware that I was totally not going to see her any time soon. I looked across at the boss and it was the first time I had seen him so happy. It was kind of creepy to think that this guy, who had been so miserable for what was beginning to seem like an eternity, was standing in front of me with a huge grin on his face.

The madness continued. Shelby and Anton gave each other high fives. I naïvely asked why they were all smiling.

'Now we know Simone was the real recipient of the drugs! You said 'Snakebite'. Do you think we're stupid? It was code. We are the snake and you have just been bitten my friend.'

What? My mind started racing. If this was what they believed, what was going to happen to Simone? When they asked her surname I genuinely couldn't remember it. All I knew was that it was an Italian name that began with an 'S'. I wanted to tell them so they could see I wasn't lying. She really was a drama student and involved with a play called *Snakebite*.

But they weren't having any of it, making arrangements for New York cops to bust Simone.

The boss turned to me and told his agents 'Right, get him out of here.'

I was handcuffed and shoved in a marked police car, taken to a small local station and thrown in a big dark cell with two local Atlanta hoodlums. I remembered it being eerily quiet and dark. It was suddenly all getting a bit scary and real. For the first time I wasn't really sure what was going to happen next but it wasn't long before I found out.

As dawn broke, I was back in cuffs and on the move, this time in a prison van, for a 45-minute transfer to Clayton County Detention Centre.

Chapter Two

CARE HOME KID

How had I landed myself in a situation where at 19 years old I was 4,000 miles away from home and facing a 25 year prison sentence and a million dollar fine?

When I've since been asked how I fell in to crime I'd say that I never fell in to it, I grew up around it. And that's true.

I was born in the East End of London where I spent the first ten years of my life with my Mum, my younger sister Barbara and older brother Eddie. My dad disappeared when I was four or five and I've never seen him since. We didn't have much but we weren't poor. I never remember going hungry or anything like that. When I was first born we lived in a flat above Rathbone Market in Canning Town. Later we moved to Beckton and then - what was to be my final family home - Brooks Rd in Plaistow.

I guess it was in my last term at Selwyn Junior School when life really started to happen to me. I met a girl at school, Nadia, and was instantly besotted.

I can still remember the day I first met her. It was the first day of term and she was walking out of the school gates to meet her mother, Angie, who was picking her up to go home at the end of that introduction to her new school.
It wasn't long before our paths crossed again at the local swimming pool and I begged my best friend, Yomi, to go up to her to see if she would go out with me. She was the first girl I had ever plucked up the courage to ask out, even if I did have to get Yomi to do it for me. She said no! Not a great start.

It wasn't until the last day of term that I finally got her to say yes. We were allowed to bring in games and I'd brought in a pack of cards. We were sitting in assembly and I pulled out the King and Queen of Hearts from the deck and showed them to her. Nadia thought it was quite a sweet thing for me to do and over that summer we spent a lot of time together.

At around the same time that I got my first girlfriend my mum had married her boyfriend, John Hicks. He was a lot younger than her, I think nearer my brother's age than hers. We never really got on and our relationship continued to worsen.

Call it a personality clash, or maybe his lack of maturity was a factor - but it eventually got to the point where I was not allowed in the same room as him. I certainly wasn't an angel, but I wasn't a tearaway either. Whenever I misbehaved I was always threatened with being put in care. One day John gave my mum an ultimatum - it was him or me. Soon there was an incident of some sort, me playing up as eleven year olds do sometimes, and the threat became a reality - my mum turned her back on me and sent me packing.

I don't remember going to the children's home for the first time, or my first night there. Surely I must have been scared or worried about the future? But looking back now, 25 years later, all I remember is being pleased to be away from the dickhead.

It was a new adventure which I took in my stride. I arrived at 80 Grantham Road, a purpose-built children's home which had an annexe at the bottom of the garden. There were at least a dozen of us, a mixed group of kids who included Billie-Jo Jenkins, her older brother Daryl and their younger sister, Maggie.

Daryl and I were the same age and we became good mates. I was in my final few months of primary school. All of us kids were taken to our different schools in a Newham Social Services minibus. Not particularly dignified!

In the coming months I went to a series of children's homes, with my few belongings in a black bin liner. I became used to moving around the care system and bumping into the same youngsters. Later on Daryl was fostered by a family in West Ham, and Billie-Jo moved to Hastings with her new family, Sion and Lois Jenkins, who coincidentally had the same surname. I never found out what happened to Maggie.

Years later in February 1997, on my way home from work, I remember seeing Billie-Jo staring out at me from the front page of *The Sun* newspaper. She had been murdered. I was heartbroken. Billie-Jo's foster dad was convicted of her murder. His conviction was later overturned on appeal and two further retrials failed to reach a verdict.

Most of the time I spent in care was at Westdene Children's Home in Buckhurst Hill, an affluent town in Essex. It was a large house on Palmerstone Road in the middle of a terrace of normal residential properties, a very nice leafy area, especially compared to East London. I saw a fair amount of Nadia in the holidays between junior and secondary school and she occasionally came to the home to see me. But her family didn't approve of her spending so much time with a boy in care. Nadia's aunt was a foster parent and they'd seen the kind of trouble older kids from the care system got in to. They wanted better for their daughter. They saw me as trouble simply because I was in a home. If her mum said she was not to see me, then she was not to see me. I didn't stand a chance.

My school life wasn't much more successful than my home life. I was going to Rokeby Senior School for Boys in Stratford. I was 13 and in my second year when another somewhat innocuous incident occurred which was to take me in another direction. My friend, Ricky, and I were on our way to an English lesson in a classroom on the top level of a four-storey block. Ricky knocked a milk bottle off the ledge and it fell and smashed on the concrete below. We were frogmarched to the headmaster's office and immediately excluded.

Another school wasn't found for me straight away and the home was at a bit of a loss with what to do with me. It was decided that in school hours, I must not be in the TV room, but should instead be in the dining room completing worksheets that someone had found for me. But the work they set was for much younger children and did not stretch me. The only thing of interest in the dining room was an old ZX Spectrum computer gathering dust alongside its manual. I asked for permission to use it and within weeks, I not only taught myself how to write my own programmes, but I found I was really good at it. If it did something wrong it was because I'd instructed it incorrectly - not because someone didn't like me, or was tired, or shouldn't even have been a social worker in the first place. I loved that computer and was very lucky that the logic of programming seemed to come naturally.

I didn't know it at the time. But by now all of the seeds of my later life were falling in to place. Growing up in the care system takes away your fear of uncertainty. Whereas most people want to have some idea of what the future holds, I think growing up in care you realise that's not possible so you embrace uncertainty because you don't have much choice. You learn to adapt to new situations and deal with whatever life throws at you.

Eventually a new school was found, Brampton Manor in East Ham. I moved homes too - to Brading Crescent in Wanstead. The home was actually a row of four terraced houses that had been connected internally to form one big building. I had a lot of fun there, mainly with two other boys my own age called Bruce and Presley. We got up to some really stupid things to pass the time.

Presley liked a dare - so we'd often mix together the most random of ingredients in the kitchen and dare him to drink it. Vinegar, Tabasco sauce, a raw egg, a squirt of washing up liquid and a squirt of mayonnaise. We never did find a combination that he wouldn't happily drink.

One evening Bruce and I were messing around and I pushed him, he fell backwards against a mirror that shattered and sent glass flying everywhere. We weren't even fighting, just messing around. It was merely an accident and fortunately no one was hurt, but the staff massively overreacted. I was told to pack my things because I was going to be transferred to a secure unit called Little Heath Lodge near Chadwell Heath, another district of East London. I was fourteen.

I was driven there by Anthony, one of the social workers I'd always liked. He'd always been friendly but for some reason decided to use the journey to try to terrify me. I'd heard about Little Heath Lodge, it was where the really bad kids were sent. Anthony put the fear of God in me by saying what the older boys did to younger ones like me. I've no idea why he decided to talk like that, and looking back on it, I realise how out of order he'd been. However, I must admit I was worried about what I had got myself into.

Unlike the other homes, which were mainly converted houses, Little Heath was a purpose-built unit, complete with barbed wire on the fences . The other boys there were all older than me and most had criminal convictions of one sort or another. There was a fair amount of violence. I managed to avoid most of it.

I had an old petty cash tin in which I stored keepsakes from Nadia - silly things like friendship bracelets and letters. It was stolen on my first night there.

Could life get any worse?

It had been spirally downwards and I was being passed from pillar to post within the care system. I was on the road to being institutionalised in my teens, with everyone telling me I was a loser, who no one wanted. But what had I ever done wrong?

It was then that an educational psychologist assessed me. His report said I would either be a master criminal or an amazing success in business. I also scored highly in the IQ test he set me. As a result, he recommended that I took my GCSEs a year early at a boarding school for gifted children in Sandwich, Kent, a golden opportunity that could have been a turning point in my life. I went as far as visiting the school and I thought it was great. The thought of being in a school environment that would be challenging and surrounded by 'normal' kids my own age was hugely appealing after only a few months at Little Heath Lodge. I said I'd love to go.

Ahead of that, though, it was decided I'd spend the remaining few weeks of the school holidays back at home with my mum and older brother. My sister was also in care by then and toy-boy John was ancient history. The best thing about being back in Plaistow was that I was around the corner from Nadia and I managed to see her whenever I could.

For the first time I was feeling optimistic about my future. I had always been an avid reader and had a good vocabulary, partly thanks to my mum. For all her faults, she was an intelligent, well-read woman and at an early age I had devoured the works of Charles Dickens. Annoyingly, at the schools and homes I'd been in, if you used words of more than a couple of syllables, you drew the wrong sort of attention. "Think you're something special do you?" Ignorance seemed something to be proud of. Thankfully, the new school was nothing like that.

Sadly, my excitement was short-lived. An argument developed over how the bill should be split for my place in the Kent countryside. As I would be boarding there, the Education Department wanted Social Services to pay a percentage of the costs. The exact amount they should pay couldn't be agreed and just as the new school term started I was told I wouldn't be going. It was a huge disappointment.

Instead, I had to resign myself to going back to Brampton Manor School for the final two years of my education. The upside was, I continued to live with mum and my brother, which at the time I thought was better than being in care, even though it could not be described as normal family life. It wasn't long before it all went wrong again.

The front room at home was quite long and Eddie had this thing where he'd run across its length and leap with a flying kick onto the sofa, even if you were sitting on it, as then you'd have to dive out of the way. One day I decided not to dive and instead grabbed his leg as it flew past my head. He fell to the floor and I jumped on top of him. I realised I'd hurt him and he was yelling at me to get off, but I knew if I got off him, I was in for a beating, so I just sat on him and refused to budge. He was screaming at me and the more he yelled the more trouble I knew I was in. I sat tight.

Unbelievably, my mum dealt with the situation by calling the police and as I was a ward of court, I was taken straight to a children's home - Grantham Road again. Daryl Jenkins was there, so it was good to see an old friend. But there was another familiar face too, Nadia's older sister, Sally. She was a year older than me, and recognised me as the boy who fancied her sister.

One evening I was sitting talking with Sally on the end of her bed. One of the social workers came in to the bedroom and I was told to get back to my own room. Not a problem. But it was reported back to Angie, Nadia's mum, that I was found "in bed" with Sally. It could have just been a slip of the tongue, but that one wrong phrase conjured up all sorts of images and killed any chance I had of carrying on seeing Nadia. Her family thought I was sleeping with her older sister and understandably wanted nothing more to do with me.

I didn't stay at Grantham Road for long. I was off to foster parents for the first time. Jacqueline and Tony lived in a smart detached home in the upmarket Essex village of Theydon Bois, nestling on the edge of Epping Forest. As well as their grown-up son and his girlfriend, they also had two other foster sons living with them.

I had free rein to do as I pleased and spent much of my time with friends in London. I was meant to be in my last year of school, but after the disappointment of not going to Sandwich, my heart wasn't really in it. I'd been skipping classes a lot and when I realised no one seemed bothered and I wasn't getting into any trouble for it, I stopped going altogether.

On my trips back into London, I often stayed at my mum's house with Eddie and a group of friends. As well as my best mate Yomi, there were Allen and Stewart Carroll, two boys we'd grown up with. Our mums had met when we were all just babies.

Mum was rarely home as she had gone back to college to study English literature. When she was there she brought back her college friends, mainly younger than her. She was trying to live her younger years again and it felt like she resented having kids around, getting in the way. Her college friends were all into smoking cannabis, even though mum herself would prefer to eat it in cookies. She told us not to call her "Mum" in front of her new friends.

It wasn't long before they were always so stoned that they would ask Eddie and me to roll their next joints. It was around this time that the two of us, along with our mates, started to smoke it ourselves. Mum wasn't fussed, they were all doing it anyway. And she took the view that it was better that we did it at home, where she knew what we were doing, than being out on the streets doing god-knows-what.

Mum eventually tired of her unconventional lifestyle and decided to pack her bags and head to New Zealand for an extended holiday. That was great for my brother. At 17 years old he had a four-bedroom house all to himself, but he was rarely alone. I stayed there quite a bit with my girlfriend, Vicki, and others regularly stayed over too. It was quite common for there to be ten of us there from Friday evenings through to

Sunday night.

Nadia would occasionally come over with her best friend, Jayne. Vicki would get really annoyed because when Nadia was in the room, she was the one I gave all of my attention to.

One day, Nadia came over to tell me she was moving. Her family were all upping sticks for Basildon. I'd never heard of it but it sounded a million miles away.

I was fast approaching sixteen, the age at which you leave the care system. Social services found a flat for me at David Lee Point in Stratford, a tower block with around 20 floors.

Together with my friend, Raymond, and my social worker, I went to buy a sofa- a black two seater with a rose design. It wasn't great but it was the only one in the shop that I could afford with the allowance I'd been given.

I asked Jackie and Tony if I could have my bedding and couldn't believe it when they said 'No'. They said it was needed for the next foster child. My social worker was shocked and told me to ask them again in front of her. So I did, and this time they said of course I could take it. I realised at that very moment they had only been in it for the money. It had not been a loving environment by any means but it had been pleasant enough. Certainly better than being in a children's home.

My flat was on the fourth floor. Thankfully, it wasn't higher, because it was one of those places where the lift was regularly out of service. I don't know what was worse, because when it was in service it stank of urine.

Regardless of its faults, I was pleased to finally have my independence and a place of my own.

Chapter Three

INTERFACE PIRATE RADIO

Once I was in my flat at David Lee Point, I wasted no time trying to get my life on track. A lot of my friends were involved with drugs - dealing them, taking them - usually both. I'd smoked a fair amount of cannabis over the past few years but I could feel it draining my energy and ambition. When I realised I was smoking it virtually every day and not enjoying it, I just stopped.

I started applying for jobs. The first interview I had was for an office junior role at a travel agents in Hatton Garden called Farnley Travel. During the interview, the owner, Leon Malmed, and his office manager, Toni, gave me a word processing test. They couldn't believe how quickly I completed it. I was hired on the spot.

I couldn't have been happier and was very proud of myself. It was a full-time position, working nine till five. I overheard a conversation about wanting to upgrade their computers to use Windows. They had to use two booking systems called Sabre and Galileo, and Toni was being told they couldn't run Windows on the computers running them, so they'd need to buy in extra machines. They were a very small firm, only about eight people and money was always tight. I told them it was possible to upgrade their machines and still run the booking systems. I was given the go-ahead to do it and they were over the moon. Leon was delighted with my work as it not only saved him a lot of money but made the organisation substantially more efficient. The only downside was that I was still on the salary of an office junior. I asked for an IT salary but Leon said the business couldn't afford it. Instead, he said if I rewrote my CV to read that I was an IT manager he would provide a reference of confirmation.

After about six months I started looking around for different work opportunities. I sent my revised CV to a number of recruitment firms and was almost immediately offered a short-term contract with the computer games company, Eidos, whose offices were in Wimbledon. I was an entry-level PC support technician and joined their small IT team. They were managed by Richard, who taught me a great deal about computer networks in a very short space of time. I was a very willing student and he was happy to spend his time on someone who was so obviously benefiting from it and grateful. With what he'd taught me, I could now get much better contracts at a more senior level.

While at Eidos, the Exchange email server kept developing problems. We worked out that the cause was a 50mb video file being shared by just about everyone in the organisation. It was a badly-animated cartoon called South Park. Of course, no one realised at the time what a huge success that one viral hit was going to become. Everyone was too busy working on the company's new game with its unrealistically proportioned heroine, Lara Croft. The game was *Tomb Raider*.

Other short-term contracts quickly followed, including stints at the BBC and Proctor and Gamble. I enjoyed the variety of work and was constantly learning all the time. I felt blessed to have a skill that I enjoyed and that also earned me good money.

A recruitment agent twisted my arm to go for an interview for a permanent role. It paid less than a contract job but would be more stable. The company was called A&G Computers, run by Ben Allen with his two partners, Martin and Phil. It was based on Tottenham Court Road in London's West End, which was the home of their main client OSI. I liked Martin who interviewed me. He was a real computer geek and I thought I'd learn a lot working with him. So when the job was offered, I took it. I was one of Ben's team of seven that supported all of the IT operations for the client.

Eddie had gone off to college to study sound engineering and was now working for a record label, Sounds of the Underground Records, or SOUR.

It was while I was working for A&G that Eddie suggested I checked out some drum and bass/jungle music websites. He gave me a list of websites, one of which was interface.pirate-radio.co.uk, a site called interFACE. I listened to a few DJ mixes and then I spotted a link labelled "chatroom", so I clicked on it. There were dozens of people in the virtual room talking to each other, mainly about the music. It moved pretty fast and it was difficult to keep up but I dived in and said hello.

They were a very friendly bunch and I logged on quite often, both at work and at home. Someone in the chatroom using the name "Brushes" showed me how to add colour and different font to my username by using HTML code. Very few people used their real name, it was all pseudonyms like AstroJax, @wiN, s p a c e, terranaut and E. I decided to use the name 'deej'. I was often mistaken for a DJ so I made a point of telling people 'it rhymes with squeege, not relay'.

Although the people in the chatroom and the listeners to the music were from all over the world, interFACE was based on my doorstep, in London. It was 1997 and one of the London pirate radio stations, broadcasting illegally on FM, had realised that broadcasting over the internet was a great way to send out their music without having to worry about the DTI finding and confiscating their transmitters. It exploded in popularity and gained a huge global following. Although it was totally legal, it kept an air of sub-culture about it. At one point someone in the States had hacked into the Tannoy system of their local shopping mall and broadcasted the station to the shoppers. The legend doesn't tell us what the residents of down-town Little Rock, or wherever it was, made of the 190 BPM hardcore gabba that interrupted their Saturday afternoon trip to Walmart.

In other parts of the world, people were picking up the audio stream from the internet and re-broadcasting it, illegally, on FM to the local area.

I was spending a lot of time in the chatroom and one of the shows I listened to regularly was Junior Buzz playing Drum'n'Bass on Saturday nights.

Eddie phoned me one evening. He was going to be DJing that weekend at a club called Happiness Stan's and he offered to put me on the guest list. I took up the offer and went along with Yomi. The club was divided into three rooms, in one of which were signs for interFACE and I realised that DJs from the station must be playing there. I went over to the door to the DJ booth and asked if Junior Buzz was around. The guy I asked was about my age. He gave me a suspicious look. 'Who wants to know?' he asked, doing his best to look menacing. 'I know him from the chatroom' I said. 'My name is deej'.

'Deej!' said Junior Buzz, as he grabbed me for a hug.

After the club, I went back to the interFACE studio. I could see why everyone in the chatroom called it "The Bunker". It was underground in the basement of an office building on Farringdon Road.

Meanwhile, Ben's firm lost the contract and he was forced to dispense with most of his staff. He kept me on but we started working out of his home in Kensal Rise. The only problem was, there wasn't enough to sustain the two of us, plus his two co-directors, Phil and Martin. He couldn't afford me and wasn't even paying himself, so I said I would go back to contract work with the promise that if things picked up for him, I would return if they wanted me to..

I became more and more involved with interFACE. I re-wrote their chat room software to make it quicker and easier to use and I developed a "bot" for the chat room, called "Pir8". If you sent a message to the chatroom and prefixed it with an exclamation mark, the bot would respond. It was used for all sorts of practical things such as showing schedules or who was currently playing, or links to archives. But we had lots of fun with it too. It ended up developing a personality of its own, complete with a bit of a sense of humour.

Even in the late 90s spammers were a problem on the internet. We'd get idiots posting stuff in the chatroom to promote things or just to be a nuisance. I enhanced the chat room software to make life harder for them. Basically, I set it up so that a tiny, virtually invisible image would show for everyone in the chat room, apart from the culprit. Instead of a harmless image, he'd get sent a huge file from NASA that would take 30 minutes to download and make the chat room unusable for him. I must admit, I enjoyed the power I gained from controlling the code of the chat room like this. But I also really enjoyed the programming side of things.

I set up my own website, info-x.co.uk, The Information Exchange, that included a discussion forum for computer security and programming related topics. I also developed a few small pieces of software and made them available from the site.

It didn't occur to me to try to charge for the software. We were in the middle of the dot com boom of the late nineties, but the whole commercial aspect of it felt like something only other people did. I assumed running a business was complicated and you'd probably only be able to do it if you'd been to Oxford or Cambridge.

My views were probably influenced by the culture of interFACE and the hacking scene - where information and music was meant to be free.

Not all of the music they played was to my taste but there were great people involved. I saw the London-based regulars - DJs and listeners - a lot, but there were always new faces too. With a dedicated following well into the thousands, London was the Mecca for interFACE listeners so people from all over the world would come and visit and hang out with us.

I became part of the bunker crew and a member of the interFACE family. Everyone involved was very passionate about the music. There was a great sense of community and some very strong friendships developed. In fact later on there would be interFACE marriages and babies.

Ultimately interFACE died because of a clash between those who wanted to keep to the anarchist roots of pirate radio and those that wanted to commercialise it. There was a multi-million pound acquisition offer that caused a huge fallout amongst the owners. But by the time that happened I'd be in a very different place.

Chapter Four

EASY MONEY

At 18 and making a little money from my programming work, I had become a minor celebrity within the interFACE community when, out of the blue, I was invited on a weekend trip to New York. Apart from a school trip to France, I'd never been abroad before - what an adventure!

My fellow travellers were sisters, Nancy and Lucy Johnson, who had both attended St Angela's Catholic School in Forest Gate. I'd met them a few years earlier at my brother Eddie's house. I'd been romantically involved with both girls at some point and got on very well with their mum, Joey, who had always been very good to me. She'd always made sure I was OK and would cook for me whenever I was there. She was like the mother I wished I'd had.

'How come he gets three sausages and I only get two?' Lucy would joke. 'He doesn't even live here!'

Lucy, Nancy and Joey were going on a shopping jaunt to New York and asked if I wanted to go with them. I had money in my pocket so… my first trip to the States. I was blown away with how new and big everything seemed: the skyscrapers, the size of the roads. It looked just like it did in the movies.

But I was missing my interFACE friends - this was the longest I had been silent away from the chatroom - so one of the first things I did was to hunt down an internet café and catch up on the latest gossip.

'Hey, I am in the Big Apple' I wrote.

A girl called Simone, using the nom de wire of "Veg", said she was also in the city. I was aware of her in the chatroom before but we'd not really spoken much. She suggested meeting later that day, so we did and over coffee realised we had lots to talk about, including our roots in England and the love of the same drum and bass music. It immediately became clear we enjoyed the banter. There was a lot of flirting. She was 20 and studying drama at New York University. Her family were from Ramsgate in Kent and had emigrated to Texas. She was a natural outdoor kind of girl: petite, slim, 5ft 7in, cargo pants, shoulder-length straight mousey hair, attractive, dressed down. Her accent made me laugh - to me she used an American accent but when talking to New Yorkers she suddenly sounded very English. It was something she continued to do for as long as I knew her.

I saw her again before I left the States and there was certainly the beginnings of a relationship.

Back in London, I was quickly in my routine of working during the day and then either in the chatroom or physically at interFACE in the evenings. Every Saturday we'd go to Happiness Stan's where Junior Buzz would play his set with his MC, MC OD. Then we'd go back to The Bunker and get drunk. Junior's real name was Kenny and his dad, Ash (aka "Mad Ash") was one of the founders of interFACE.

Junior had got together with a girl from the chatroom called Angel, real name Lin. Their relationship was getting pretty serious. Seeing them together somehow made me think more about Simone in New York, with whom I'd kept in touch via the chat room and on private chat using something called ICQ, which was the instant messenger service popular at the time. We spent hours talking, we just clicked and got on really well. I was spending so much time talking to her through the night that I was beginning to get into work late. I've never been great at getting up in the morning, but staying up till 3am certainly didn't make it any easier. Eventually, Reuters got sick of my poor timekeeping and cancelled my contract.

I wanted to make another trip to New York to see Simone, so the last thing I needed was to lose my job.

One evening I was with Allen Carroll. Although we were similar, he was much more of a jack the lad. I was a little bit more sensible, while he hung around with some of the dodgier people we knew who I would do my best to avoid.

After leaving school, Allen had become a trainee chef. We spent many weekends together and had often smoked weed but then he started experimenting with cocaine, which I didn't want to get involved with.

When I told him I was going to New York, he stopped me in my tracks.

'I'll be there, too!'

We laughed and I said: 'Why? What are you doing there?'

I wondered how a trainee chef could afford to go to New York. He was hardly a globetrotter.

'Don't worry about it. But we should meet there' Allen assured me enthusiastically.

So I let Simone know I'd be meeting up with a friend in New York. She arranged for one of her pals to make up a foursome for a night out. Allen and I travelled on different flights - he'd already booked his ticket by the time I reserved mine. When I got to New York, I met him in his hotel before we were due to hook up with Simone and her friend Natalie. I was shocked to see stacks of dollar bills in his room, and on the bedside table was a load of ecstasy tablets. It didn't take a second for the penny to drop. Everything fell into place.

'Now I know why you are out here' I said, matter-of-factly.

Allen was a middle-ranking coordinator in a drugs ring. He travelled without drugs but met two runners in the hotel who had brought the gear over from England. They would then all meet an American buyer, who handed over stacks of cash. It was Allen's job to take the money safely back to the UK in hand luggage.

Nothing more was said after that brief explanation and we made our way to the club with the girls. I knew the people he mixed with, so wasn't surprised he was involved with dealing drugs. I'd sold a little bit of weed when I was younger but dealing ecstasy internationally? That was a whole different game.

We had a great weekend. Simone and Nat took us to a club called Concrete Jungle - people were breakdancing to Drum'n'Bass which you just didn't do in UK clubs. Same music, different vibe. Allen didn't hit it off with Simone's friend, Natalie. An English guy came up to me and said he'd instantly spotted that my mate was from across The Pond.

'How?' I asked.

'Reebok Classics' he pointed at Allen's shoes, 'and a Ben Sherman shirt. Basic uniform innit?'

We got chatting but Allen started annoying me. He was doing his usual thing of trying to give the impression that he was a bit of a gangster. He loved it.

I stayed the night with Simone at my hotel. We got on really well and we agreed we'd see each other again soon.

Meanwhile, back in England, I had to face up to some hard facts. I was fast running out of money after losing my contract. I had no cash reserve — I had spent it all in New York, happy to splash it on having fun with Simone. I was talking to various agencies. Reuters had been paying £45 an hour but I was being offered £25, maybe £30, and was holding out for better. There was always an agent with a better paid contract for which to interview soon.

I couldn't pay the rent and, worse still, I couldn't see when I would be able to afford to go back to New York. Allen was at my place one evening with a bottle of Jack Daniels and told me he was going back to New York for one of his trips.

I was intrigued by the mechanics of the venture but at the same time, appalled at how much they were paying for their airline tickets. I knew I could save them money by buying them through my first employer. Leon, the boss at Farnley Travel, had been good to me so putting some business his way seemed the right thing to do.

'We can only book one of the two tickets through them though,' Allen said. 'You have to make sure there's no connection between the two couriers, so that if one gets stopped they don't realise the other one is connected to him. Separate tickets, check in independently and they don't talk to each other either at the airport or during the flight.'

I was intrigued as we talked about the different ways the couriers took the drugs out. Checked-in luggage was apparently a bad idea - more thoroughly inspected than hand luggage. So the pills were put into rolls and hidden in talcum powder bottles and portable speakers.

'Getting the gear out there is actually the easy bit' he said 'These bloody Yanks insist on paying with $20 bills. $100k in twenties takes up a lot of space!'

'So you have two people taking the drugs out to split the risk, right' I said, an idea starting to take shape in my head as I was talking. 'Why not have two people bring the cash back? As well as reducing the risk, you also spread out the bulk.'

'Yeah, totally' said Allen as he cut up another line of coke. 'But who can you trust with that kind of cash?'

'Let me pour you another drink' I smiled.

So, it was agreed. I'd get an all-expenses-paid trip to New York, enabling me to see Simone and have enough cash to pay the rent and a bit to spare. It made perfect sense.

Anyway, in my mind, I was going to do it only the once as a quick solution to get me out of my financial troubles. And then I would be on to my next contract.

The following weekend we headed out to New York. Simone was delighted to see me and we made the most of our time together. She didn't have a clue about the drugs.

My last night in New York was a heavy one and I was woken up the following morning by Allen banging on my door.

'Mate, we're gonna miss the flight - sort yourself out!'

Simone was in bed with me. I had about 10 minutes to get up, dress and get out of the room. And the one thing I absolutely couldn't forget was the $50,000 hidden behind the curtain. There was no way I could get to it without her seeing.

'Don't ask me any questions and I won't have to lie to you' I said.

'What are you talking about, Duane?'

I repeated my warning. 'OK' she said hesitantly. I grabbed the money and started stashing it into the back of a pair of portable speakers that I planned to take in my hand luggage.

The $50,000 is rolled into tight tubes, secured with rubber bands.

'I'm not even going to ask!' she promised.

We kissed and hugged and went our separate ways, then Allen and I dashed to the airport by taxi. We were booked on different flights to reduce the risk of being caught together and I left on an earlier plane. At Heathrow, I was met by Lee and Andy, part of our group and who I had known since childhood. Lee was what you'd call "a face" in our area - someone everyone knew and commanded a lot of respect. He was about four years older than me, not big-built but with an air of menace about him that was really disconcerting. Andy was his right-hand man and had been for as long as I could remember. He used to live a few doors down from Allen and his brothers in Canning Town

Rain poured down as we drove back on the motorway, heading for my flat. Lee drove, while I was in the back. Andy had the speakers and with was dismantling them with a screwdriver to remove the cash which he then passed back to me. I took off the rubber bands and was trying to flatten out the dollar bills under my thighs.

'I'm sitting on a fortune!' I joked.

Then we heard a police siren behind us. We had $50,000 in our possession that we couldn't account for. Lee stopped the car and two police officers came to the window.

Looking in on the three of us, one asked: 'Do you know why we have pulled you over?'

My heart was pounding.

'Yes, because we are international drug smugglers' I wanted to say.

'You're not wearing your seat belts, lads' explained one of the policemen.

They asked Andy and Lee to step out of the car to give their details. Although he'd been driving for years, Lee had never bothered to get a driving licence, so he gave his name as Chris Carroll, Stewart and Allen's older brother. I heard the small talk from my seat in the back of the car as I sat on the cash. Andy explained they'd just picked up their mate, me, from the airport after a holiday.

The policeman opened my door and beckoned at me to get out of the car too. I knew the game was up. As soon as I stood up the dollar bills were going to fly all over the southbound carriageway of the M25.

I was resigned to being caught red-handed. Just as I was about to get out of my seat he said 'Don't worry. You've probably been in a hot country and we don't want you getting all wet and cold, do we?'

Then, rain pouring off his waterproofs, he crouched down next to me and took my details. His face was inches from the money. My heart was still pounding, everything racing through my mind.

The officers went back to their car to run our details through the computer. Andy was convinced Lee had given the wrong year for Chris' date of birth. In the mirror, we could see them on the radio as we tried not to panic. As the officer walked towards us, we were certain it was all over. 'Nice knowing you both,' said Andy in a failed attempt to lighten the mood.

You cannot imagine the sheer relief when the cop said to us 'On your way lads. Don't forget to wear your seat belts.'

We couldn't believe our luck and said a prayer to the patron saint of drug traffickers - if there was one - and drove back to London. Obeying the speed limit and with our seatbelts on.

Needing to get the dollars converted to Sterling, a bureau de change in the West End was the next move after freshening up at my place. I changed $9,000, keeping it below the $10,000 threshold that we knew would trigger an NCIS (National Criminal Intelligence Service) report, and was dropped back at home. They took the rest of the dollars which they were going to get changed later: In all, it took 12 transactions to launder the money. I was pleased I wasn't involved in any further risk. I'd got my money and was happy. Job done.

Now I had to look around for a contract but I was becoming half-hearted in my search. At the back of my mind, these New York deals were an easy way to make money and I wasn't hurting anyone. You just walked through Customs and it was pretty straightforward, wasn't it? London to New York was a pretty safe route in the eyes of Customs, so they just didn't bother stopping people.

Within a month I was discussing doing another trip. We had our orders to hold off for a while as one of our drugs couriers had lost his bottle and backed out. In stepped Duane Jackson, wannabe drugs smuggler. I was desperate to see Simone. It was January and I hadn't seen her since before Christmas. I was 19, impulsive and impatient. We were young and starting to fall in love.

'I will take the drugs' I said. 'It's easy.'

Taking drugs out was a lot more nerve-wracking in practice than it was in theory. The day before my flight, Lee dropped off a rucksack containing 6,500 ecstasy tablets. Some were already secreted in the speakers, others hidden in talcum powder containers.

I was not aware of the seriousness of what I was doing. I didn't think of ecstasy as a dangerous drug. It's not like it was heroin or cocaine, which I wouldn't have touched with a bargepole. Everyone was taking ecstasy on the London club scene. Except me - it didn't appeal.

If I got caught it would have been a slap on the wrist, wouldn't it? Ecstasy was just a party drug, surely? No, like heroin or cocaine, it's a class A drug. But I didn't know that at the time.

I was due to get paid a little more for this trip because I was actually carrying the drugs and not just bringing back the money. There was no risk to me. Nobody knew who I was, they said.

Nevertheless, I didn't sleep too well that night. It must have been nerves. I was jittery for the whole uneventful flight. As I turned to walk through Customs I was relieved to see no officers waiting for me but still I held my breath as I walked through the 'Nothing to Declare' lane.

I picked up a payphone to call London.

'Just letting you know I am in New York for the weekend.' Code for "I made it!"

I met Allen at the hotel and he went off to change some money. I spent another great weekend with Simone. She was well aware that something was going on but didn't seem too bothered by it. Her family were of Italian extraction and her father was supposedly a waiter in a restaurant although Simone implied there was a Mafia connection. She didn't ask any more questions of me and so I didn't of her.

Allen came out with me to see Simone and he wanted to be The Big I Am – very flash and revelling in the gangster/drug smuggler image, although he never openly said what he was doing.

Back in England, Lee and Andy were on hand to pick me up at the airport and drive me home. I was relieved the operation had passed off without incident and I was even more keen to know when the next trip would be. I wanted to go as soon as possible as Simone wanted me to see a play in which she was involved, *Snakebite*, opening off Broadway.

'I'll do this again' I thought. I had actually stopped looking for new contracts by now. I knew it was wrong but I still didn't think what I was doing was that serious. It was all quite casual and as far as I was concerned, easy money.

Allen had started coming out with my friends from the interFACE crowd. And he wanted to be the centre of attention to try to pick up girls. I found it all a bit cringeworthy and wished he would be more discreet — but that was Allen and he was my friend.

My relationship with Simone was getting more serious and I was starting to look at getting contracts to work in New York. I mentioned it to her and she was excited at the prospect of us being together on a more permanent basis.

* * *

It's now May, 1999. I've got a drugs run to the States tomorrow but tonight I'm in the pub with friends from interFACE - Lin, Elise and Edwin. We're in the infamous Blind Beggar in London's Whitechapel, where Ronnie Kray shot dead George Cornell. They know I am off the next day, what I am doing, and are genuinely worried for me. Edwin jokes that he hopes the pedigree of the pub we've ended up in isn't a bad omen. I am still quite blasé about the whole thing but their concern has got me thinking for the first time of the consequences of what I am doing.

I'd never really given it much thought before. It had all happened quite quickly and easily. I hadn't given much thought to the possibility of being arrested It may have "only" been Ecstasy tablet, but it was still drugs and there were some seriously dodgy people involved on both sides of the Atlantic. Ending up like George Cornell with a bullet in me didn't seem so implausible after all. I decided there and then this would be my last trip. I never intended to have a career as a drug smuggler.

As well as the concern from my friends, a sudden change of plan also unnerved me.

A week earlier, just before we were booking the ticket, Lee phoned to say that the American buyer would be down south on business and wanted to do the deal in Atlanta instead of New York. I nearly pulled out there and then - why the hell did I want to go to Atlanta? Simone was in New York and she was the only reason I had got myself into this, not to spend a long weekend in a moody bed and breakfast in a state I'd barely heard of.

After a bit of negotiation, they kept me on board by offering more money to cover the extra internal flights. I'd land in Atlanta, do the deal, then hop on a domestic flight to New York in time to see the play *Snakebite* with Simone. All expenses covered and a little extra thrown in for the inconvenience of it all.

What could possibly go wrong?

Chapter Five

CLAYTON COUNTY
DETENTION CENTER

And so we return to where you found me. The drugs run to Atlanta ended badly with me being arrested. And after an eventful evening with the DEA I was taken to Clayton County Detention Center on the outskirts of Atlanta, Georgia.

I walked solemnly into the modern building, still handcuffed to my police chaperone. Last night's escapade felt like a lifetime ago and reality was sinking in. Once in the prison I was un-cuffed and I began the long process of being checked in.

There were about a dozen other guys going through the same process, a mix of races and ages, although most of them were in their late twenties. You could tell some of them were old-hands at prison formalities.

Sliding electric doors and thick glass windows were everywhere. The process of going from the front gate to the main body of the prison seemed very efficient. Almost like a factory line. Thankfully, given my state of mind, it wasn't too taxing. I just did as I were told.

I was ordered to take off all my clothes. I was standing stark bollock naked while I took my turn in a glass-sided cubicle to be hosed down and sprayed with anti-lice powder. I was given a regulatory red jumpsuit to put on and then directed into a big room with benches along the sides where others were sitting awaiting further processing. But there was a big difference between them and me. My jumpsuit was red, while they were all wearing blue. Everyone else noticed this too.

I quickly felt a sense of intrigue and respect. Here was a guy with a red jumpsuit. And it was not long before one of my new fellow inmates broke the silence and asked what I was in for. I explained I was caught with drugs coming through the airport. He threw back his head and laughed, saying it must have been one huge fucking bust because I was heading for maximum security. It was at that point that I realised the significance of my red jumpsuit. I was being sent to B1 Pod, a particular wing of the prison.

I was given bedding and a small bag containing toiletries. The prison officers were known as bulls or COs - Correctional Officers. One of them, a woman, escorted me to the door of the pod and a huge, daunting sliding metal door opened.

'In you go, honey' she said.

As I took those few feeble steps across the threshold it dawned on me that I was in a proper prison for the first time in my life. And a whole heap of trouble. The door swished closed behind me, like something out of *Star Trek*, but much noisier.

No-one noticed my arrival. Or if they did, they weren't interested. For one thing, everyone was wearing a red jump suit here, so I no longer stood out. I presumed I was going to be allocated a cell but there were no COs anywhere to be seen, just a whole load of scary-looking guys in red jumpsuits.

What was I going to do? Stand there paralysed with fear or get on with it?. Get on with what though? I walked further into the pod to try to take in my surroundings. It was a huge expansive room, that felt a bit like an aircraft hangar, shaped like a triangle with one of the corners chopped off. So there was a long wall and a shorter wall facing each other - the door I had just come in from was at the shorter end. I was facing the long wall at the other side of the pod, about 25 metres away. It had two floors of cells against the big back wall and was obviously overcrowded. There were probably three times the number of inmates it was designed for. I counted only about 20 cells, but there were a good 30 or so single mattresses on the floor at the far end of the room. And between me and the mattresses were, metal benches and tables firmly anchored to the floor. There was also a bank of pay phones to my left, none of which were being used.

Halfway up the shorter wall was obviously a section of one-way glass, from which, I figured, we were being watched.

Some people stood in groups chatting while others were laying on their mattresses, many reading. Some sat at the benches playing cards. The black-white ratio of prisoners was probably 60-40, with a few Hispanics thrown into the mix.

I was at a total loss as to what to do. A prisoner brushed past me and told me to find an empty mattress and get comfortable. I just nodded in thanks at the advice, found an available one, put down my belongings, such as they were, and sat, trying to adjust to what was going on around me. I knew I had to be on my guard. This was heavy stuff and I was thinking survival. I was certainly not thinking long-term. The next 60 minutes were what I was worried about, not the next 60 days - if I lived that long.

One of the first things to hit me was the distinction between the older prisoners and the younger ones, who were quite rowdy. A few were even rapping Tupac Shakur songs – my kind of music. At that moment I wanted more than anything else in the world to have a shower. But the reputation of what went on in prison showers meant that I was not going to chance my luck. Instead, I decided to try to get some sleep.

I woke up what could have been either five minutes or five hours later when I sensed movement around me. Everyone was headed to form a queue near the benches where food was being dished out. I registered with thanks that I hadn't been raped in my sleep and got up to join the queue. The food was being served from big metal containers and ladled into bulky but lightweight yellowish plastic trays with compartments moulded into them. I ate my food - I had no idea what it was. Then I went back to my mattress and slept again, although I kept waking up through the night as I didn't feel particularly safe. The next morning I felt more alive and sat taking in what was going on around me. I asked someone where the shower was and he pointed. Was I brave enough? No, not yet.

One of the older black prisoners noticed my English accent and caught my glance. He came over to me and introduced himself. It was apparent that he was the boss of the pod. His name was Joel. No mattress on the floor for him - he had a proper cell.

'You're English. Where from? London?'

From that moment on he called me London, as everyone else soon would.

He invited me to sit and talk with him and to play chess on one of the metal benches. Joel was a nice guy. 'Avuncular' was the word that sprang to mind. Although he was a big guy and certainly seemed to command respect from everyone around him, he was not intimidating to me. For the first time I was able to relax a little but there was no letting down my guard. I was something of a novelty and, with Joel's approval, other prisoners started coming over to me and asking about life across the Pond.

One guy wanted to know if we had black people in London.

'Sure we do' I told him.

'What about cars? You got cars?' He wasn't even joking.

And of course, they all wanted to know if I knew the Queen. They wanted to know what crime I had committed and I explained I was caught trafficking drugs.

'You're a big man in London?' asked one of the younger guys.

'Nah, not really' I said. But they thought I was playing it down. 'Yeah, you a big man in London, London!'. They'd seen the movies. English guys were the bad asses, the uber villains. Word went around that I was a big-time London gangster and not to be messed with, which I found really funny.

Joel explained how the phones worked. They only functioned at set times when the bulls turned them on. You dialled the number you wanted and an automated system called the number and asked if they would accept a reverse charge from a correctional facility. If they accepted then you had your call.

As soon as the phones were enabled that evening I jumped on one and tried to call Allen back in London. But it kept telling me the number wasn't recognised. Eventually I worked out that they just weren't set up for international calls. Who could I call in the US? Simone? But I didn't know her number by memory and my scrap of paper with her phone number on it was long gone. Probably sitting on some DEA agents desk, forming part of the case against me.

The following day I was playing cards with Joel and talking about the comical situation that happened at the hotel. He loved the story. Someone came over and asked 'Hey, London - you got *showers* in London?' and ran off.

I still hadn't had a shower since before going to the Blind Beggar in Whitechapel, a million years ago, and I was starting to stink. So I finished my game and headed for the showers. I'd seen where they were - I'd just not had the guts to go in there.

As I went through the door where I'd seen people go to shower, I was relieved to see that it was just a group of four single-person cubicles and not the big open-plan rape chamber I was expecting. And I was the only one in there. While having that first shower felt so good, there was a downside to it. I don't want to be too explicit here but you've got a bunch of men locked up in a prison. In the showers they get naked and have a bit of privacy. Let's just say I was doing my best not to touch the walls or the layers of slime on them.

Next evening I was lying on my mattress and a older white inmate, Charles, challenged me to a game of chess. I'd already clocked him as being a bit of an oddball, not least because he'd been sitting on his mattress praying and reading the Bible out loud in the evenings. He was very intense but I couldn't see any harm in a game of chess. I enjoyed kicking his ass and when he immediately demanded a rematch I did it again. I was pretty pleased with myself but he was starting to get annoyed, my cockiness beginning to piss him off.

'Three - nil' I smiled. 'You're not very good at this are you?'

Another prisoner pulled me aside and warned me to calm down.

'You really don't want to annoy him. He killed three people last week, including a little kid, and an old woman. That's why he's in here - waiting to go to court' he explained.

Shit!

'Watch yourself, he has a screw loose' he warned.

I played four further games of chess with Charles and I let him win every time. I never played him after that. Hearing him praying at night was even creepier once I knew what he'd done.

On day three, with the help of a CO, I managed to place a call to London, phoning Allen's number and he accepted the reverse charge.

I was relieved to hear his voice and he explained that he knew I had been arrested. But very quickly Allen's voice changed. He warned me that even if I had the chance to return to London I should stay away.

Worse was to come.

'You'll be shot as soon as you leave the airport' he told me. Clayton County Jail was suddenly an appealing option.

Allen explained that within hours of my arrest the entire gang in London had received a visit from the police. The first question they were all asked was 'Do you know Duane Jackson?'

Allen knew I hadn't grassed them up. But how else had they collared all the right people at the right addresses? How had the police been so precise and quick?

Mutual friends who had not been involved in the operation had not had their doors kicked in, so the finger of suspicion was pointing squarely at me.

The whole gang was arrested and on bail. Police had even smashed into my flat and taken away my computer.

Allen also had some news from my sister, Barbara. Back home I had owed my mum £400. Being in debt to her was one of the deciding factors to do the drugs run. I would have had enough money to repay her and get her off my back. My mum was due to meet the police at my place a couple of days later so that they could give her access to the flat. She told them about the debt and shamelessly bragged that she planned to sell anything I had of value to recoup the money I owed her.

Even the police thought this was a bit harsh so they arranged with Barbara for her to go to the flat the day before my mum so that she could empty it of my belongings and keep them safe.

Barbara said the officers recognised her as she walked towards my flat. But how would they have known who she was? Barbara thought it strange. Allen agreed.

What Allen had told me left my mind racing. I was confused and slightly dumbfounded. It was not what I had expected to hear. It was obvious that the safest place for me at the moment was where I was now. I was grateful for my mattress on the floor.

* * *

One afternoon towards the end of my first week, three black guys were jumping around, laughing and rapping a Tupac song but, infuriatingly, they kept getting one of the verses wrong and it was really annoying me.

'It's not like that, it goes like this' I told them. It wasn't one of my best thought-out moves.

The fun in them disappeared instantly. They weren't laughing any more. 'What do you know, white boy?'

The mood turned decidedly dark. But before it could escalate, Joel coolly stepped in to diffuse the situation. I had been in there less than a week and already I was barely managing to stay out of trouble.

There was a strict no-smoking policy in American prisons, so I'd gone from my usual 20 a day habit to none - at a time when I could probably most do with them. An inmate had smuggled in a stash of tobacco but they hadn't managed to get any rolling papers. Undeterred, they used pages from the Bible - a book easily available in Southern prisons and printed on very thin paper. I was invited to join a few guys for a smoke in a corner that was something of a blind spot, out of sight of the bulls. I was looking forward to my first smoke but it was disgusting. Two puffs were all I could manage and after that I just let the other prisoners get on with it.

Once a day, the bulls entered the pod. We had advance warning and were ordered to sit on our hands on the floor. They checked out what they wanted to see and then left. But apart from this routine I never saw them. Prison life was run by the inmates. Meals were taken on a giant trestle table at one end of the room. Breakfast comprised of milk and cereal. It didn't look appetising and I never bothered. Grits was the main dish and the only drink was iced tea, which I had never previously heard of. I was popular because I never ate my full portions and prisoners were more than happy to take my leftovers. For lunch it was grits with everything. It was the same again every evening. The food was disgusting. Even the bread was yellow.

From talking to Joel, I realised that I was in maximum security for my own safety. The alternative was a pod which was home to street thugs and much more violent. I was caged up with rapists and murderers awaiting trial and very long sentences. They had done their crime and were now trying to be on their best behaviour so they would get good reports in court to help with sentencing and hopefully be sent to a good prison. This was considered a safer environment and in a bizarre way the authorities were looking out for me.

He explained I would soon be taken to court within the prison for a hearing with a state-appointed lawyer and, as if on cue, I was told the lawyer was here to introduce himself. I'd seen what others did when they had to leave the pod and I followed suit. I stuffed my meagre possessions into my pillowcase and left them with Joel to look after. I went to see my lawyer for a very short meeting prior to the court appearance due the next day. It was just a formality, he said, there was no need to go into any detail or worry about a defence or plea just yet.

'That'll be months away' he assured me. Oh, great!

When I got back to the pod there were a group of white prisoners, all covered in tattoos, standing over my mattress. One of them asked me why I was 'running with the brothers'.

'If you want your stuff looking after, you give it to us, your own brothers. Not the niggers. You stick with your own' he explained, menacingly.

Stupidly, I hadn't realised the prisoners had segregated themselves according to race. How could I not have noticed that I was the only white guy in Joel's group?

My court visit came and went. It was a non-event. I had to sit and wait to be given my next date before I had any further clue as to what my fate would be.

While I wasn't as terrified as I was when I first came in to the prison, it still wasn't a nice place to be. I was missing home, my friends, English accents, decent food, a bed! I was taking it one day at a time.

Word of where I was being held started to spread back home and I started to get the occasional letter. I even got a love letter from Nancy, saying she hoped that we could have been together. I later found out that Joey had contacted my Mum to offer her help to try and get me out but was greeted with the response: "It's where he was always going to end up; leave him there."

Back to reality, Joel confirmed what Agent Shelby had already predicted - that I was most likely facing a 25-year prison term. Twenty-five years of this? It was too daunting to comprehend. Lying on my mattress, I wondered how it had all gone so horribly wrong. Everything had been going so well for me, apart from the hiccup over the contract money.

* * *

Towards the end of my second week, we heard a shout from behind that imposing metal door that the bulls were coming into the pod, so again we had to go through the ritual of sitting on our hands on the floor. Two bulls, one of them a woman, walked alongside my mattress. I expected them to carry on past me. I had done nothing wrong. But she stopped next to me and handed me a piece of paper, turned on her heels and walked back out of the pod.

The note contained a London number and read: 'Call Ben Allen.'

After I stopped working for Ben, his business had continued to go downhill. His two co-directors went and took jobs, so it was just him. I occasionally helped him out when he needed me for some kind of techie task that was beyond him. But he wasn't someone I'd class as a friend. Just an ex-employer that I occasionally spoke to.

The piece of paper totally confused me. He had no connection with the drugs operation. How would he even know where I was? And if he'd found out then surely I was the last person he would want to hear from?

But I was excited at the prospect of hearing a friendly voice and so, even though it was to take a few days to organise another international call, I asked the bulls to help me. I was apprehensive about speaking to Ben but this quickly faded to relief as we started to talk. He explained that he had not been able to get hold of me for a week and had gone on the interFACE website and into the chat rooms to ask if anyone knew my whereabouts.

People there were initially cagey as they had no idea who this guy was. It probably didn't help matters that he'd opted for the screen name 'Shag'. But one of the interFACE crowd checked him out and realised he was who he said he was and told him what they knew.

When he found out, he acted swiftly, contacting the prison to see if he could speak to me. He had even found out the amount of my astronomical bail setting – $50,000 – and that only payment of the full amount would secure my release on bail.

Ben asked if I wanted his help and said he had a proposal for me.

'Yes, please' I said. Obviously.

When talking to interFACE fans in the chatroom he had come across an American girl called Stacey (screen-name: "Space") that I had met when she had visited the bunker during a trip to London. She lived in New York and helped him find where I was being held and to navigate the American justice system. Ben said that the two of them would visit me in Clayton County to discuss how they could get me out. Two days later, they arrived. I was allowed only one visitor, so Ben came in to see me

It was so good to see a friendly face. If it wasn't for the thick glass wall between us I think I would have kissed him!

Stacey waited in reception as Ben outlined his plan via the telephone behind the glass wall. He had already spoken to the DEA and on payment of the full bail money I would get my passport back, allowing me to return to London and await a trial date, which was going to be at least a year away.

Ben explained that he would put up the money but I would have to go back to court whenever asked so he would not forfeit the money. He would pay the bail on condition that I lived and worked with him during that interim 12 months. He said he'd pay me a reasonable salary and that when I was eventually called for trial in the US that I would appear and face the consequences.

Without hesitation, I agreed. He was offering me a year of freedom. I was even excited at the prospect of returning to England and thinking of home. Joel was on hand with even more advice and said that if by some miracle my bail could be met, it should be paid to a bondsman to guarantee the money being returned. If it was paid into the court, it would be lost: when it came to sentencing, I would be fined as well as thrown into jail. The fine would coincidentally be the same as the bail money and Ben would never see his $50,000 again.

I advised Ben of Joel's wise words, then he and Stacey proceeded to max out all their credit cards and call on all their savings to raise the money.

The next day I waited for my freedom. I said goodbye to the few people I'd got to know and thanked Joel for looking after me and wished him the best. I finally heard my name being bellowed out and I walked through the sliding door to be processed out of Clayton County.

Getting out was almost as tough as getting in. There was a strict process to follow. One by one I had to hand over the items I was given when I came in.

'Towel?' Check!'

'Pillow?' Check!

I was almost jumping up and down with the excitement of soon being back in the fresh air.

'Blanket?' Check!

Burger King - I'm sure I saw a Burger King on my way here. Anything but grits!

'Face cloth?'

'Errm, no. Sorry - haven't got that.' I patted the pockets of my red jumpsuit to show I wasn't trying to smuggle a flannel out of the prison

'I must have lost it' I explained.

'Can't let you out without you returning your facecloth.'

And with that they turned me around and escorted me back into the pod.

I was dazed, standing back inside the pod that I thought I'd just left for good. Did that really just happen?

Joel came straight over to me to ask what the hell was going on. He saw the devastation on my face, as I explained I'd been sent back over a stupid face cloth, which I had obviously left somewhere and which was now standing between me and freedom. He gave me his with the words: 'Go home, London'.

It was the last time I ever saw him.

Chapter Six

A STAY OF EXECUTION

I was out in the fresh air and finally rid of the red jumpsuit I'd been living in. Ben was waiting for me, along with Stacey and, to my total surprise, Simone was there too

Stacey lived in Rochester, in New York State. She'd picked up Simone en route via New York City. It was so good to see them both. We had a big embrace and there were hugs all round. A real sense of victory. Although of course it was only a stay of execution. I was so pleased to have my freedom back. Ben had booked a hotel for the night for us and I couldn't wait to spend time with Simone.

The first thing I needed was a cigarette. I hadn't smoked the whole month that I was inside - apart from the incident with the Bible. I should really have given up there and then but smoking again felt like me reclaiming my freedom. It tasted awful but I still never gave up. The four of us had a celebration meal and then back at the hotel the comfortable bed looked so inviting, particularly after that mattress on the floor.

My time with Simone was to be short-lived as Ben had booked our flights for the next day. I was filled with relief at heading for home even though I still had a massive prison sentence hanging over me. But I had a year of freedom and I was so grateful.

The consensus was that I had been a bloody idiot. Ben said if I had needed money I should have gone to him and asked for it. Ben's background could not have been more different to mine. He was middle-class with a good education and had grown up in a solid, loving family environment. He was the only boy, with a number of older sisters. Coming to my rescue had been an incredible act of kindness. The interFACE community had also been pivotal in getting me out of jail. It was in the chatroom that Ben had found out where I was and the fact that Stacey had helped showed the power, close bonds and friendships the network had helped to create.

Although obviously relieved to be out of prison, I still had a big problem. Ringing in my ears was Allen's warning that everyone in London thought I was a grass. I still hadn't told Ben that I could be facing a load of trouble if I went back there. I knew I had to phone Allen. 'I'm coming home' I said. 'I've made bail.'

'Good timing, you're in the clear' he told me. He wasn't emotional about it. He'd known all along that I wouldn't have grassed. He explained that the guy I knew as Tony - Dylan, the ringleader – had gone on the run as soon as people started getting nicked in London. As I was being released from Clayton County Jail, he was getting arrested on a plane trying to leave Amsterdam. There's no way I could have pointed the finger at him - I didn't know his real name, never mind where he was. What finally put me totally in the clear was Dylan's solicitors finding out that we had all been under surveillance for six months. That also explained how the police had recognised Barbara when she went to my flat. She had been seen with me when we'd been under watch.

Everyone who had been picked up in London was released on bail. Apart from Dylan. He was kept in prison on remand because he had been caught while on the run. Importantly for me, I was clear to return home without worrying about the consequences.

Ben lived in a four-bedroom, end of terrace house in a leafy street in Kensal Rise, NW10. It was a world away from the East End where I'd grown up. I'd been there before when he'd used it as his office after losing the support contract in Tottenham Court Road. It was eerily quiet compared with the buzz of the West End. There were no staff and he'd lived alone since his divorce.

In Atlanta I had agreed to report to the UK police when I got back to London. I didn't have much of a choice - it was a condition of getting my passport back from the DEA. I'd been told to go to Bishopsgate Police Station, the home of the City of London Police, a force totally independent of the Metropolitan Police, which is responsible for Greater London. It never occurred to me or anyone else at the time, but it made no sense that these guys were the ones on our case. Investigating drug trafficking should have fallen to what was then called Customs and Excise.

It wasn't for at least another year before we realised this and worked out the implications: There had been a multi-million pound investigation, going on for about one year, covering two to four trips a month, involving thousands of ecstasy tablets. Dylan was bringing them in by ferry from Amsterdam and then on to London. Amsterdam to the US was classed as a dangerous route, while London to New York was less risky. Couriers would meet the ferry and bring the tablets by car to the capital. Lee ran the London end. He organised the couriers to go the States to take the drugs out and bring the money back. Dylan would have lined up the buyers in the US.

I had no idea of the extent of this operation. Even so, I wasn't too worried about visiting the police station. I was already facing charges in the US and I'd been assured by the DEA that I wouldn't be charged separately in London. I was met by DCs Timmins and Chidgey. How wrong could the Americans have been? I was promptly arrested.

It was totally unexpected and Ben, who had come to the station with me, was pretty pissed off. I had a duty solicitor and thankfully he advised me to give a 'no comment' interview. If you ever find yourself unexpectedly arrested you really want a solicitor who will tell you to say 'no comment'. If a solicitor has advised you to do that then it can't be held against you at trial, whereas if a solicitor tells you to answer the questions but you instead say 'no comment' throughout the interview then this can be held up in court as a sign of your lack of cooperation. So after merely confirming my name and address I answered 'no comment' to every question. The officers explained that they were going to get an administrative dismissal of the charges in the US so that they could charge and try me in the UK with the others they'd arrested. This was brilliant news. Not only did it mean that Ben would get his bail money back, it also meant I'd be serving my sentence in an English jail instead of in the States. Even better, the sentence was sure to be much shorter. I was facing up to 25 years in Atlanta. But here I'd only get 16 years - maybe even 12 if the judge was in a good mood. I was 20 by now, so I worked out that with time off for good behaviour I'd easily be out of prison by the time I was 30. Result!

I was released on bail and as part of the conditions I had to sign on at the local police station every couple of weeks so that they knew I hadn't disappeared. I arranged to get myself a proper legal brief and signed up with John Zani, who was based in London. He was incredulous at our first meeting. He did a double take when he saw me and I asked him why he looked so confused. He said that after looking at my name and the charges he'd fully expected me to be a six-foot black guy.

The charges against us all were finally formalised. There was the drug trafficking charge as expected: 'Conspiracy to Export a Controlled Drug of Class A'. But changing the money from US dollars to Sterling was an offence in itself - money laundering, or 'Conspiracy to Convert own Proceeds of Drug Trafficking'.

Conspiracy charges are incredibly difficult to defend. You don't even need to have done anything to be found guilty. If two or more people agree to commit a crime at some time in the future then that's a conspiracy. Just knowing about it can be enough to get you convicted on a conspiracy charge.

As I was the only one caught with any drugs, there was an extra charge just for me: 'Knowingly concerned with the export of controlled drugs of class A'. This related to the single incident when I was caught. There was no way I could get out of that one, so I decided to plead guilty to it.

I thought it'd be hard for the prosecution to prove my involvement beyond that one incident so I was going to plead not guilty to the other two charges and fight them out at trial. All my co-defendants did the same.

The rest of the gang were a mixed bunch: Dylan Lowry was the lynchpin between the UK and US. It was his arrest on the plane in Amsterdam that earlier put me in the clear. Dylan was from the Isle of Man, university-educated, well-spoken and in his late 20s. You'd never suspect he was the mastermind of a drug trafficking ring. He was in HMP Brixton awaiting trial while the rest of us were on bail.

Lee Barclay, the top man in the London operation, was quite chuffed when the court case was tabled as 'Barclay and Others'. He got top billing while we were all relegated to be labelled as 'others'. Lee was your archetypal East End geezer. What he lacked in physical build he made up for with an air of menace that came effortlessly to him.

Andy Lattimer, at 26, was number two in the London organisation and Lee's right-hand man. A smart cookie, whose biggest strength was letting people think he was stupid. Later on in court, when he was asked to swear to tell the truth, he made out he couldn't read the card with the wording on it.

Lee Smith, 23, was not the brightest bulb on the Christmas tree. He had been involved as a courier and when the police went to arrest him he was living with his mum in Canning Town, east London. During the raid, the police found his mum's heart tablets on the sideboard and confiscated them in case they were part of the haul. The police allegedly threatened to implicate her by swapping her heart tablets for Ecstasy unless he gave a full confession. They said that if he didn't admit to everything, then they'd say that he was the ring leader and he'd get a very long sentence. He gave a full confession on the spot. He later retracted it when he realised that his confession was the only evidence against him.

Amanda, Dylan's girlfriend, was the only female in the group. While Dylan didn't fit the mould of a crime kingpin, Amanda was everything central casting could ask for in the role of a gangster's moll. She was exactly the kind of woman you would expect to be the girlfriend of an international drugs trafficker. She was 24 and a former lap dancer. Blonde, tanned and toned.

Gerald was Dylan's best friend. I'd never met him before and he kept his distance from the rest of us.

The eighth and final defendant was Paul Strachan. He was a young guy and had couriered drugs just the once. I'd not met him before the trial and felt a bit sorry for him as he was clearly way out of his depth.

Allen and his older brother Chris had gone on the run and hadn't yet been charged so wouldn't be standing trial with us. They spent the next year based in Ibiza continuing to move drugs around Europe.

It was the summer of 1999 when I was arrested in London and the trial was set to be held at Southwark Crown Court in June 2000, so I had a year to wait. It was a strange position to be in. I had my freedom but I also knew I was going to stand trial and that I would be going to prison. The only unknown was for how long.

I worked with Ben throughout that year. He converted the largest bedroom in the house into an office with four desks, even though there was just the two of us. The business was still based around supplying hardware and installing and supporting networks. But the work just wasn't coming in. One of Ben's clients needed a website hosted so I suggested we got a server and host it ourselves. We both knew our way around managing a web server and it was a lucrative business if you could get enough clients. Re-focussing the company on web services - hosting, design, development and streaming media - proved to be a good move and we started to get really busy.

I wasn't interested in the business side of things, like dealing with accountants, suppliers and paying bills. I enjoyed the technical stuff - programming websites, managing the servers and stuff like that. And there was certainly enough work to keep me busy.

Streaming media proved to be popular. We hosted two online radio stations. Stage4.co.uk was run by Steve O'Hear, now a well-known TechCrunch writer. The other was Pyrotechnic, similar to interFACE, broadcasting online urban music.

Six months into the bail and just as we approached celebrating the Millennium, we received word that the charges in the States had now formally been dropped so I could stand trial in the UK. Importantly, it also meant that Ben's bail money would now be released. His business had been turned around and I was working flat out, a valuable distraction from bigger worries.

Ben would take regular trips sky-diving in France and had bought a new BMW M3. I never did get the salary I'd been promised when he bailed me out. He told me the business could not afford to pay me. I suppose things could have been a lot worse, though. I had a roof over my head and food in my stomach. And I wasn't in an American prison.

Occasionally I'd manage to get a tenner from Ben to go into central London and see my friends at interFACE. My mates there looked after me well and there was never any shortage of weekend fun to be had. It was widely known that I was awaiting trial and this gave me a kind of celebrity status, a notoriety that seemed to attract women. Things with Simone had cooled rapidly during my time on bail. She was in the States, I couldn't visit her and I had a big sentence hanging over me. Ultimately the relationship fizzled out, although we remained good friends.

After a night out at a club, usually where one of our group was DJing, we'd all head back to the interFACE studio - 'The Bunker'. After Junior Buzz and MC OD broadcast their set we'd all chill out. Somehow we'd manage to fall asleep at about 3am while DJ Switch was playing his happy hardcore set at full volume.

The webmaster at interFACE was a real character, known just by the letter E. He was about 20 years older than me and had certainly enjoyed a colourful life. He had a really bad scar down one arm. The story behind it was that he fell asleep against a radiator one night and was so off his face on drugs that he didn't feel his arm burning.

E told me not to worry about prison, that I'd actually have a lot of laughs in there and I wouldn't believe the fun things I'd end up doing. I thought he was crazy. Well, no. I *knew* he was crazy - I just thought he was talking nonsense about prison. How could you have 'fun' in prison?

I celebrated the Millennium with a whole crowd of interFACE friends on London Bridge. It was the last big celebration I would have and we partied all night. I have vague recollections of handcuffing someone to a bus stop.

Within the year, Ben brought Stacey over from the US. She played up the stereotype of a loud American and she was very much loved by most of the interFACE crowd. Ben and Stacey started a short-lived relationship and she did some design work for our clients.

Two weeks before the trial was due to start, Ben called me in to the front room of the house. He had a number of contracts on the table and a bottle of champagne. Stacey was with us. He explained 'Because I have not been able to pay you a salary and you are going to prison for a long time, I want you to have something to look forward to when you come out. I am going to give you 20 per cent of the company.' It took me completely by surprise. I wasn't expecting it. I didn't really understand the details of the contract that was called an 'Option Agreement'. He said all I needed to do was sign and I was then officially the owner of a fifth of the company. I signed and and we cracked open the bubbly.

I was happy that the hard work I had put in to turn the business around was being recognised. And he was right, it helped to have something to look forward to beyond losing my freedom.

Chapter Seven

A STAR PERFORMANCE

I hadn't seen much of my co-defendants early on in my bail period, although at one point I had been for a drink with Lee Barclay. I was in the unique position of being the only one caught in possession of any actual drugs. And so Lee turned to me and said 'It will be a lot easier for everyone if you didn't stand trial. I'll give you £10,000 to disappear and not turn up.'

It didn't take much thought to turn it down. My first concern was that Ben would lose the money he'd put up to bail me out of prison in the States - he hadn't got it back by that point - and I would have had to have spent my life on the run. I said I would rather not live like that and would have to take what was coming. I turned down his offer. He said it still stood if I changed my mind.

I was occasionally in touch with Allen too. Someone appeared in the interFACE chatroom with the screen-name of 'Chef', asking for me. It took me a while to realise it was him as he was being so cryptic. But once we'd figured out that it was a pretty secure means of communication we kept in touch that way. As I had written the chat room software I was able to get his IP address and worked out that he was in Spain.

In the run up to the trial, we all met up to talk tactics. The only one missing was Dylan, who was on remand in HMP Brixton.

The intention was to get our story straight. We didn't want to be pointing the finger at each other in court. Lee chaired the meeting and did an excellent job of keeping everyone in line and we all went away confident that our stories would be consistent.

The fact that Allen and Chris Carroll were on the run worked perfectly for us. Lee came up with the story that the London ring was run by the Carroll brothers and they intimidated everyone to take part. The beauty of the story was that they weren't there to defend themselves. For anyone who actually knew Allen and Chris, the suggestion that they'd intimidated anyone would have been laughable. But the jury didn't know them, so we could paint whatever picture we liked.

There was some worry that Dylan might 'turn QE' (Queen's Evidence), meaning that he might appear as a prosecution witness against us so that he could get a lighter sentence. In the ensuing fall out, he and Amanda split up. She became very flirty with me but I took it as a joke as I thought she was way out of my league.

I met my barrister, David Martin-Sperry. I was pleading guilty to the one charge of being "knowingly concerned", so there was nothing to do regarding that but await sentencing. That would come after the outcome of the trial to determine my guilt on the two conspiracy charges to which we were all pleading not guilty. The story was that I made only one trip that had anything to do with the drugs operation. Beyond that I knew nothing about it. The barrister was keen to play the "rose between two thorns"- defence. He'd been an advisor to Lynda La Plante on the *Prime Suspect* TV series and had developed a liking for theatrical defences.

Developing my case with David, I explained the other trips had all been to see Simone and were completely innocent. He felt it would be helpful if she give evidence on my behalf. My problem with the idea was that she knew about the cash behind the curtain and certainly had some idea of what was going on. It wouldn't be fair to put her in that position so I said it was unlikely she would be willing to travel to London to appear in court.

Although he said it could mean the difference between prison or freedom, I didn't want to ask her to commit perjury for me, even if it meant me going to jail.

As it happened, Simone came over a few days ahead of the hearing so that we could spend some time together before I started my inevitable prison sentence. I met her at Heathrow and was taken aback when with her on the Tube, she said 'Not long till the trial. What do you want me to say in the witness box?'

I realised she was a drama student and she saw it as her first big acting role. She was loving it all. She wanted a starring part. I couldn't believe it and couldn't wait to tell my barrister.

I had been facing a 25-year sentence in the States but I was now looking at a 12 to 14- year stretch. Not great, but better than America. All of us that were due to stand trial feared the worst and it we knew there was a high chance that these would be our last few weeks of freedom. We made the most of it and went out quite a few times as a group. I suspect Lee wanted to make sure we were all going to toe the party line. Amanda was coming on to me much stronger and Lee was winding me up about it. He said 'She really likes you.' I thought she was just messing with me but one night we got a bit drunk and ended up in bed together.

In a morbid way I had been looking forward to the trial. I was keen to find out how long my sentence would be so I could start serving it and know when my life would get back to normal.

I didn't have to wait long.

* * *

All criminal trials follow the same format. First, the prosecution presents its evidence and then the defence responds. One of the key pieces of evidence against me was the phone call I'd made to Simone from the hotel in Atlanta when I was with the DEA. A transcript of the call had been submitted into evidence but it wasn't a true account of the conversation. The DEA claimed I'd phoned Simone, shouting as soon as she answered 'Snakebite, snakebite, snakebite!' and she'd hung up. This was totally fabricated and completely ridiculous. I knew that the call had been recorded, so I asked my barrister to request the tape. The DEA said they'd lost it.

We managed to get the judge to kick out the transcript so it couldn't be used against me. But when I was in the witness box, it was clear that they thought Simone was involved. They said that they'd tried to track her down but I hadn't been truthful in the information I'd given them about her. I'd told them her first name but that I couldn't remember her surname. All I could remember was that it was Italian and began with an 'S'. I'd told them she was a drama student at NYU. The DEA claimed they'd tried to find her but had failed.

The suggestion from the prosecution counsel was that I had made her up and given her a false name and that, in fact, she was the contact person in the States to whom I was delivering the drugs.

He turned to the jury and said that, rest assured, she was involved and if the US agents could have found her she would also have been in the dock. Sitting down, he looked pleased with himself for having seemingly torpedoed part of my defence.

My barrister then called our first witness, Simone Scarnera. There was an audible buzz of excitement around the courtroom. I looked at her as she walked into the courtroom. She was in her element, as if starring in a scene from a tense Hollywood courtroom drama. Simone, with her Italian sounding surname, was about to steal the show.

She took the stand and confidently lied through her teeth, saying she had no knowledge of any drugs and had no reason to suspect I was involved in anything illegal. For the whole period of all of my trips she could account for my time.

My barrister thanked her for her time and said, tongue in cheek 'I hope you have all your affairs in order because you are now going to be arrested for your part in this alleged criminal organisation. The prosecution said that you would have been arrested if you could have been found.'

But in reality his learned friend just stood up, meekly uttering 'No further questions' before very quickly sitting back down.

The judge was clearly annoyed by the dramatics but also slightly amused. I was delighted as it felt as if we'd scored the first goal. Simone was elated. 'You're free to go' she was told and she gave me a knowing smile as she walked slowly out of the courtroom. Exit stage right.

I was in the witness box giving evidence for three exhausting days. I stuck to my story, that I didn't have a clue about what was going on until a week before my ill-fated trip to Atlanta, which had been organised after I had met up with Allen. He revealed what he was doing and in a moment of weakness and because I was short of money I stupidly agreed to get involved.

Whenever the prosecution counsel asked me a question to which I couldn't remember the answer or didn't want to answer I'd say "I don't remember"

"You don't remember or you won't remember?" he constantly repeated. I was hoping for some verbal jousting but in my somewhat biased opinion the guy was annoyingly inarticulate and not very bright. Most of the time he just resorted to sarcasm and knowing looks thrown at the jury.

My co-defendants handled themselves with varying degrees of success. Lee Barclay told tales of intimidating gangsters in blacked-out BMWs who had forced him to cooperate. He said he refused to name them for fear of the repercussions. Throughout everyone's defence was threaded the suggestion that the fearsome Carroll Brothers - Allen and Chris - were the real masterminds behind the operation.

Lee Smith's barrister tried to get his confession kicked out. If he'd succeeded, then Lee would have walked away scot free as there was no other evidence against him. But he failed and Lee climbed to the witness box to explain how the police had made him confess by threatening to implicate his mum and pointing the finger at him as the ring leader. It sounded about as plausible as Lee Barclay's story with the difference being that it was true.

The evidence against Gerald was very thin and he said he hardly knew "these other people" who were in the dock with him. That wasn't totally untrue. He did a good job throughout the trial of making sure he didn't talk to the rest of us in the dock and sat as far away from us as possible. He was actually Dylan's best friend and right-hand man, who worked with him on the Isle of Man. He scrubbed up well, as he stood in the dock all suited and booted.

We all thought we had done reasonably well. I was resigned to a custodial sentence for the charge I had admitted. It was a question of how the jury would view me on the other two counts.

After seven weeks of evidence and defence, the trial was finally over. The jury retired to consider their verdicts while we retired to the pub to get absolutely hammered.

Back in court the following day, we just sat and waited for news that the jury had reached a verdict. It felt like the longest day of the trial. Nothing at all happened, the jury hadn't yet reached a decision.

On the second day we were called back into the dock because the jury had a question relating to me. They wanted to know that given I had already admitted to involvement on the one charge relating to a single incident, how could they determine if I was guilty of the other two conspiracy charges?

The jury was sent out of the courtroom and a debate started. It was agreed between the barristers and the judge that if the jury thought I was aware of anything going on before that night with Allen then they should find me guilty. If, however, they thought I only knew about it from meeting him on that night I was not guilty of the conspiracy charges.

I was very happy about this. The jury had taken their responsibility seriously and there was some doubt in their mind whether I was guilty of these charges. It felt as if there was a real chance I would be found not guilty and get a much shorter overall sentence.

The jury was called back in to be given the answer to their question. But when the judge stared to direct them, his comments didn't bear any resemblance to what had been agreed. He simply said that if they thought I was involved or aware beyond that one event they should find me guilty. I desperately tried in vain to attract the attention of the junior barrister who was sitting in on my barrister's behalf. I couldn't very well start shouting from the dock, much as I wanted to. I was left fuming and suddenly worried as the glimmer of hope I'd had seemed to have evaporated.

The public gallery was full for the entire trial. Ben and Stacey were regularly there to support me, along with many of my friends from interFACE.

The jury went out again and we were told the verdicts would be handed down the following day.

Gerald's fate was delivered first - not guilty on both counts. That raised our hopes. But they were only to be dashed again when every other charge against the rest of us was guilty.

It was still a blow, even though I knew it was coming. We were taken downstairs to the holding cells to be remanded in custody and await sentencing in five weeks.

We knew the guys would be transferred to Brixton, with Amanda going to Holloway. As Dylan had not been on bail, he was quickly sent back to Brixton Prison,while the rest of us had to be processed as new arrivals.

Lee reckoned that although Dylan hadn't turn Queen's Evidence the fact that he was prepared to could prove a problem. He warned that we should be prepared for it to all kick off as soon as we got into the wing. He expected us all to watch out for him and be prepared to get involved when he dealt with Dylan. This left us in do doubt about what he was going to do.

I wasn't scared about going to prison or my safety inside. I was with a gang of tough guys and we were in it together. It couldn't have been any worse than those dark days in Clayton, where I had been so alone.

While we waited for the prison van, Lee turned to me and said 'What are we going to do about your name?'

'What do you mean?' I asked.

'Well, I'm not calling you "Deej". What kind of name is that? And Duane ain't that much better'

I just laughed. I'd got to know Lee well enough over the past few months that I understood his sense of humour.

'Derrrr-wayne Jackson' he mused. 'I know - Jacko. Right, listen guys - from now on, he's Jacko' he said, pointing at me.

Chapter Eight

GOOD LUCK, BAD LUCK

We didn't have long to wait in the bowels of the court.

Eventually, we were collected in a prison van with blacked-out windows. Each of us was locked into our own cubicle with our own thoughts. It wasn't a long journey, but it was a very quiet one. As we drove along Tooley Street, away from Southwark Crown Court, I gazed out of the window. Again I felt that sense of surrealness I'd had back in Atlanta. It was a beautiful sunny day outside and everyone was just going about their business as if nothing significant had just happened. But here I was, inches away on the other side of the tinted glass on my way to start a long spell in prison. I knew I wouldn't be strolling freely out in the sun for quite a while.

It didn't take us long to arrive at Brixton Prison and to be admitted. Thankfully, the process was a far less humiliating ordeal than in the States. The prison itself couldn't have been any more different. While Clayton County Detention Center was very modern, HMP Brixton was nearly 200 years old and it showed. Still, I knew where I'd rather be now.

'All ready to say hello to Dylan?' Lee asked as we were led on to "A" wing, which housed about 100 other inmates. The group of us were strolling along together, chests out like strutting peacocks, swaggering and ready for a fight.

We soon spotted Dylan, who stood out from the crowd of other inmates because of the chef's whites he was wearing. It wasn't fancy dress, so we knew he must be working in the kitchen where his duties included serving up the food. He spotted us and I could see he was nervous.

Lee stopped and turned around to face the rest of us. 'Might be best to keep him sweet' he said. He'd decided it would be better to stay friendly in the hope of getting bigger servings of food. So Dylan's bacon was saved by, well, bacon. Instead of a beating from Lee and the boys, he was met with a hearty slap on the back. I was relieved, I'd rather not be caught up in a fight - especially not in my first hour in prison.

I left Lee and Dylan to catch up and went to find my allocated cell.

'Excuse me mate' I said to a prison officer 'Where's cell number 9?'. He slowly leaned towards me and put his face right in front of mine. Our noses almost touching.

'I'M NOT YOUR FUCKING MATE!' he bellowed. 'YOU WILL ADDRESS ME AS SIR OR GUV.'

Blimey! I wasn't going to make that mistake again.

I managed to find my cell without any assistance from the friendly screws. Although we had all been sent to the same wing, we were in different cells, each with two people, so we all had unfamiliar cellmates. I must have drawn the short straw.

My cell mate was an older Algerian man who spoke little English, meaning we hardly exchanged a word. This language barrier caused problems early on in our short stay together. It was one night in my first week, we'd been locked up for the night and I was on the top bunk writing a letter.

All of a sudden he jumped out of the bed below me and, without a word, turned off the light.

So of course I got off of my bed and turned it back on - I pointed at my pen and paper and tried to explain that I was still writing.

As soon as I had climbed up on to my bunk he got up and turned silently turned the light off again. So I turned it back on again and turned to him showing my fist.

I don't know much Arabic but I was pretty sure that the words he spat at me weren't ones he'd use in front of his mother. But he left the light alone until I turned it off myself an hour or so later.

The cell door was unlocked at about 8.30am and he immediately shot out, leaving me to get up and brush my teeth in peace. As I was doing so, I glanced in the plastic mirror above the sink and noticed a group of 12 scary-looking Algerians gathering near the door. They clearly wanted to pick a fight.

They all spoke pidgin English but one in particular spoke more than the others and started to translate. They were asking me why I had threatened the old man. I explained that he kept turning the light off while I was trying to write. They slowly closed in on me and the situation became increasingly tense, with voices starting to be raised.

I backed in to my cell. There was nowhere to escape to - the only exit route was the cell doorway in front of me but this was blocked by an increasingly angry mob of Algerians. This wasn't going to end well. Suddenly there was a shout from behind them: 'Oi!'. As the Algerians fell back, my six co-defendants were standing there behind them. And next to them were their cellmates who had come to help as well. 'You all right, Jacko? Is there a problem here?'

As the Algerians realised I was not alone and my friends didn't look like the kind of people they wanted to mess with the atmosphere changed. They visibly crumbled, knowing what was good for them. 'No problem here' one of them said, holding up his hands in a gesture of surrender. The translator was keen to make sure my friends knew he was just a translator and not looking for trouble. The leader of the Algerian gang insisted on shaking my hand to show everyone that we were really the best of friends and that there must have been some sort of misunderstanding.

I shook his hand but shrugged out of his attempt to hug me.

The old man moved into another cell and was replaced by Paul, a big black muscular guy from Sierra Leone. We got on fine and would listen to his music tapes, mainly stuff by the American reggae group Morgan Heritage, to which I still listen to now, but outside the cell he kept to himself. He said the worst thing he ever did was to build himself up because everyone wanted to fight the big man to prove how hard they were. In reality he just wanted a quiet life. I heard much later that Paul eventually lost the plot and was found in another cell trying to eat the floor tiles. I'm sure he'd been through a lot in Sierra Leone and wasn't coping with prison too well.

* * *

We were all waiting for sentencing to give us some idea of how long we'd be inside. There wasn't much to do. Exercise was for about an hour a day in the big courtyard but other than that and mealtimes, we'd be locked up in our cells.

While there was a prison library, it was very hard to get in, due, I think, to prison overcrowding and staff shortages. There was a box on the wing for returning books, so I often scavenged whatever I could. I went to grab a book at the same time as an inmate who I could only think would have been a Hell's Angel on the outside. He was the kind of guy you'd cross the road to avoid on a sunny afternoon, never mind on a dark night - or in a prison. But we got chatting and it turned out he was a really sharp guy and very well read. That experience, together with the one with my cellmate, Paul, taught me never to judge a book by its cover. Neither were anything like I'd have assumed they were just from looking at them.

In the evenings I wrote letters, which helped pass the time and it was good when I got a few back. Nights were frustrating as it was hard to sleep with all the noise. There was a lot of shouting between cells which seemed to go on until morning, so I spent a lot of time awake with only my thoughts for company. How long could I put up with a regime of no sleep and being locked up for nearly 23 hours a day? At least in the US we had the run of the wing. The only thing that kept me going was knowing that once sentenced I would be moved to another prison where life would be a lot different. I prayed for sentencing day.

It was interesting to hear of the different prisons called when people were being moved on. From the reactions of the departing prisoners you could work out the reputation of the jail where they were heading. It quickly became obvious that the last place you wanted to go was Camp Hill on the Isle of Wight.

Finally, about six weeks after first arriving at HMP Brixton, sentencing day arrived and we were driven back to court. This time I did my best not to look out of the windows at life passing me by. I thought it would only get me down, so why bother? I was already withdrawing myself from the outside world - something everyone in prison does in order to get by. Once at court, we were taken down to the cells and found Amanda already there, having been transferred from Holloway women's prison.

She'd somehow got her hand on some powdered Valium and managed to get some over to our cell. Lee and some of the others snorted some, but I passed up the offer.

Our barristers saw us briefly and gave the same message: Expect a sentence of between 12 and 16 years.

Eventually we were all brought up to the dock for sentencing. There was a lot of preamble and I just wished the judge would just get to the nitty gritty of how many years I was going down for. If you thought your sentence was too harsh you could appeal against it, so judges list all the things they have considered to reduce your scope to appeal. Judges don't like their decisions overturned on appeal.

I could tell by the way the judge was now talking that sentences were about to be given. He said he'd been surprised at how young we were to be operating at this level. Normally gangs of this sophistication were in their late 30s or 40s. While the guidelines dictated we should be sentenced to 12 years each, he took our youth into consideration and said that was to be reflected in the sentences he was about to give us.

The moment of truth arrived: Dylan got nine years for conspiracy to export a Controlled Class A substance and conspiracy to launder the proceeds of drug trafficking. He was screwed from day one in terms of perception with the jury. While we walked in from the public area of the court, he was brought up from the cells, implying he had been refused bail. So he had a huge hurdle to climb in the minds of those judging him.

Lee Barclay was handed down six years. Then me, described in court as a willing lieutenant, five years.

The judge went on: Amanda and Paul, four years each. Lee Smith got the same sentence, even though the only piece of evidence against him was his confession, which his solicitor tried to get dismissed.

Drug charges against Andy were thrown out for lack of evidence and he was convicted on just the money laundering offence and got two years.

I couldn't believe my five years. What a result! We were all expecting much more. The dock erupted as we all hugged each other like we'd won the FA Cup. Our friends and families in the public gallery were confused by our joy and looked upset. The judge called for order and we were sent down to the cells to await transfer back to prison.

I'd learnt a lot about prison sentences in the preceding few weeks. If you got less than four years you were automatically released halfway through; four or more years meant you were eligible for early release on parole halfway through but not guaranteed to get it.

In the van returning to prison I worked out my earliest possible release date. Assuming I behaved myself and got parole at the first opportunity, I'd be out in two and a half years. December 9, 2002. Two Christmases and three birthdays.

The journey passed in silence. Everyone was making the same calculation. That was when I realised that the phrase 'doing time' is literal. That's all you do in prison, count down the time to a release date and find things to try to make the time pass quicker. All you're doing is time. Tick, tock. Tick, tock.

Back at Brixton, we were left to wonder where we would be sent.

Prisons and prisoners are divided into categories. Category A is high security - places like Belmarsh - and Category D is open prison, like HMP Ford. We knew that we were all Category C prisoners, so had a rough idea of where we could end up and our prison of choice would have been HMP Coldingley, which had a good reputation among inmates.

That evening as I sat in my cell, I began to wonder about the fact that we'd been investigated by City of London police and not Customs and Excise. With sentencing out of the way, I must have had more space in my head to think about other things. Allen was the younger of the Carroll brothers and Chris the eldest but there was a middle brother, Stewart. There was no other way of putting this other than saying Stewart was an idiot. A plonker. Not harmful, malicious or nasty. Just a bit of a doughnut. He'd been caught with his hand in the till at his office in Moorgate, right in the centre of the City of London and the police were called. Although Stewart wasn't involved with the drug smuggling, he certainly knew about it, thanks to Allen's big mouth. I wouldn't have put it past him to have told the police all about it just to avoid getting a caution for stealing from his employer. The more I thought about it, the more I became convinced that this was the only way we could have ended up with City of London police on us instead of Customs and Excise. Stewart had grassed us all up, including his two brothers. It was the kind of stupid thing he would have done.

I discussed my suspicions with Lee Barclay, who said he had been thinking along the same lines. 'I don't want us to influence each other' he explained, grabbing a pencil and paper. 'Write down the name you have and I'll do the same.'

In silence we wrote on our pieces of paper and swapped them. I unfolded the one Lee had written on: "Stewart Carroll".

After that we didn't have much more time to discuss it as we were being locked up for the night in our separate cells.

Next day, still on a high from our lenient sentence, my name was called out, along with Lee Barclay and Lee Smith. 'Bad luck guys, you are off to Camp Hill' we were told. 'You have an hour to pack.'

Chapter Nine

MY NEW HOME

HMP Camp Hill is based in the centre of the Isle of Wight, off the south coast of England. We were taken there in a prison van, possibly exactly the same vehicle that had taken us from court to HMP Brixton.

Aboard the Isle of Wight ferry, crossing from the mainland, we were kept locked in our tiny cubicles in the prison van, Lee, Smithy and I, and a couple of other prisoners. I shouted out 'What if this sinks?'. There was a fair amount of banter in the van - I guess it was our way of keeping our spirits up. We saw everyone else's reaction when they were sent to Camp Hill and we knew we didn't have much to look forward to there.

Arriving at the prison, I remember thinking how clean and civilised it was compared with Brixton. Camp Hill was more modern, particularly the reception wings. Like most prisons, there was an induction wing. St. Andrew's Wing was where new prisoners started off and learned the rules of the prison and how it all worked.

It struck me how quiet it was at night, again in contrast to the noisiness of Brixton, which was quite threatening.
On the induction wing you also had the opportunity to look at what you wanted to do - the work you might apply for or any educational courses. The best paid job was in the kitchens at £20 a week. It had its perks, including the obvious access to more food. The downside was that you are working with inmates from Parkhurst and Albany - the two neighbouring prisons on the island. Parkhurst is for people serving long sentences, Ronnie Kray spent time there. But Albany is a sex offenders' prison and so you would be working alongside rapists, paedophiles and other sex offenders.

It sounded like too much hard work for me and I didn't really want to be mixing with this type of person. Sex offenders really are the lowest of the low. People genuinely loathe them and if there is even the slightest rumour of you being one you are likely to be attacked, which I saw happen in Brixton. Hot water and sugar in a Thermos flask is thrown in the face. It can scar for life.

I wanted to do an IT degree and thought the best way to get started on that route would be to apply for the education department. So that's what I put on my form.

We were told by fellow prisoners that St. Thomas' was the drug-free wing and was the best one we could get. We were told that it was more sought after than the main two wings - St Georges and St Michaels - because it was more modern and was a little more relaxed. It was supposedly meant for addicts who wanted to get clean. You had to agree to random testing, which didn't bother me because I didn't take drugs. The appeal was that it was a slightly smaller wing and cleaner, a little nicer, less aggravation and violence.

Drugs are a big problem in prison. Outside of prison, heroin users are seen as scum even amongst other drug users. We'd agreed that we wouldn't associate with anyone using it. But we quickly realised that if we stuck to that rule then we wouldn't have many people to talk to because so many prisoners were addicted to the drug. The three of us - me, Lee and Smithy - liked the appeal of being on a wing without the junkies, so we all applied for St Thomas' Wing and were relieved to be accepted.

'Welcome to the drugs-free wing where all the drugs are free' joked one of the other prisoners. He was only half joking. There were as many drugs on St Thomas' wing as there were elsewhere in the prison. But most of the prisoners had found ways around the random drug testing.

The cells on St Thomas' Wing are mainly four-man cells. It's more desirable than a two-man cell as you're less likely to be stuck on your own with an idiot. It's better to spend time locked up with three other people than just one.

My application for the Education Department was accepted and I started a course called CLAIT - Computer Literacy and Information Technology. The four-week course was a very basic introduction to IT, word processing and spreadsheets. I couldn't resist showing off and I completed it in one day. The teacher, Ian Gutteridge laughed and asked if I'd mind helping out some of the other students who were struggling.

* * *

I quickly settled into the routine of prison life at Camp Hill. The day would start at about 8am when the cells are opened up. You're given cereal and milk the night before so breakfast is eaten in the cell. You're also issued with a Thermos flask so usually there'd be people running around in the morning filling up their flask, borrowing tea bags and getting ready for the day.

At 8.30 those that are working the morning shift head off from the wing to education or whatever workshop they're working in. If you're not working in the mornings then you're locked up until lunchtime.

At midday the cells are opened and the morning workers return to the wing where lunch is served. Every week you're given a sheet of paper with multiple choices for food for each day. It doesn't matter what you choose. All of it is as bad as the rest. You tick the boxes and hand in the form. The food is all cooked in a central kitchen and brought to the wings in huge metal trays. It's then served by the six inmates on the wing who have the job as orderlies.

You all queue up for your food and take it back to your cells which are left unlocked for about an hour or so while people are getting their food and eating it.

At 1pm the cells are all locked while the screws have their lunch. At about 2.30 they're opened again for the afternoon workers to go to classrooms and workshops. They return at 5.30 and dinner is served in the same way as lunch. You're then locked up again.

Then, it's the highlight of the day - "association". At 7pm all the cells are opened for about 90 minutes and you all head downstairs to mingle. It's during association that you can grab a shower, make a phone call or play pool.

At 8.30pm we're all locked up for the night. This ritual usually takes a good 20 minutes for the screws to get us all locked up because everyone is running from cell to cell borrowing music or tea bags or filling their flask.

We'd spend the rest of the evening watching TV. *The Sopranos* were a big favourite and, it goes without saying, virtually every prisoner loved their football, except me. Then we would go to bed to start all over again the following day. Doing time.

That's how it worked for the vast majority of inmates. However, each wing had a small group of orderlies. They're prisoners that are trusted a little more and are responsible for cleaning and painting the wing, running the wing laundry, serving food and so on. If you were an orderly then you had free run of the wing for both the morning and afternoon sessions. That meant that you could take a shower or make a phone call without all the other prisoners around. It was a coveted job because you'd get so much freedom and also get a two-man cell, shared with a fellow orderly, so you were with a better class of prisoner.

I'd been told pretty categorically that there was no way I'd be able to do any sort of degree in prison as I had hoped. It was just not geared up for it. They covered basic literacy, numeracy and IT skills but not much else. Even an Open University course wouldn't be possible.

So I stayed on in the education department helping to teach the CLAIT course with Ian in the afternoons. Ian was very good to me. I remember he'd occasionally bring in chocolate for me or CDs that friends of mine had sent to his home. I don't think that I appreciated at the time how big a risk he was taking for me. He could easily have lost his job if he got caught. There was an obvious "them and us" in prison, the prisoners and the screws. Teachers fall in the middle somewhere as "civvies", but they were much more seen as "them" than "us".

This caused me a bit of a problem. I had a difficult balancing act to make sure I wasn't seen as getting above myself and acting like I was a teacher or thinking I was somehow better than my fellow prisoners. That would have been a dangerous position to be in. But I was aware of the situation and I managed to get the balance about right. The inmates genuinely wanted to learn about this "computer stuff". I think most of them thought it would be a passport to computer crime and that on the outside they would be able to hack into banks instead of doing street robberies.

In the mornings I'd stay in my cell and read or sleep. You try to sleep as much as possible in prison as it helps the time to pass. I'd also do the occasional bit of programming, but not in the usual way. I'd write PERL (a programming language) scripts with pen and paper and post them out to Ben to be typed up. I'd then phone him in the evenings to go through any problems and suggest changes over the phone to get it fixed.

The time spent being locked up wasn't too bad. I was in a four-man cell with Smithy and Lee Barclay and one other. So it was like being in a really awful bed and breakfast with your mates. We'd play cards a lot. Kalooki, a Jamaican version of rummy, is very popular in prison. We'd been taught lots of the prison tricks, so we'd occasionally be brewing prison hooch and getting slightly drunk. The three of us formed a close unit, always looking out for each other and it was very difficult for the fourth person in the cell. They'd come and go pretty quickly, usually having asked the screws to move them on. They were always going to be the outsider.

We'd sometimes joke about escape plans and work out how it might be possible to break out. The problem was that we were in the middle of an island. So even if you could get through the concrete walls of your cell and over the razor wire fences, you'd still need to get to a port and off the island before you were missed and the authorities alerted. There are some beautiful places on the Isle of Wight. HMP Camp Hill isn't one of them.

* * *

Lee Barclay and I got on really well and grew closer over the time we shared a cell. We realised that we'd actually briefly been in the same children's home many years before. We had a lot of laughs. Smithy was a different character. He took himself very seriously and was incredibly tight. Lee or I would run out of cigarette papers and have to borrow some from other cells (and pay 100 per cent interest), only to find out Smithy had five full packets stashed under his bed.

There was a standard banking system in all prisons in the UK. The currency was phonecards and tobacco. Both a 20 unit phone card and a half-ounce of tobacco cost around £2 so they're used interchangeably. There's also a default interest rate that's fixed at 100 per cent, known as "double bubble". Basically, if I lend you a phonecard, you have to give me back two. It's not seen as extortionate, it's just the way it is and widely accepted.

There were also a few scams, and Lee and I became quite good at one of them. It's called "shaving cards" and involved phone cards which are incredibly low-tech. There was a white stripe on them that was stamped by the phone each time you used it. Each card had 20 units of credit on it. Someone had worked out that if you shave a fraction of a millimetre off the edge of the card it effectively resets it so you could use it again for another 20 credits. But you had to do it before you used the final credit. So you effectively got 39 credits out of a 20 credit card. If you shaved off too much, then it wouldn't work. Lee and I were quite competitive about who was better at shaving cards and a lot of the others on the wing would come to us for help to get it done. It's not as easy as it sounds and it's also illegal. We were defrauding the phone company.

Everyone knew the three of us were co-defendants, or "co-d's" as those inside shortened it to. And because there were three of us we never had any trouble. I became quite a bit cockier than I would otherwise have been, because I knew the Lees were there to back me up if I ever had any problems.

We learnt how to manage prison life together. One incident sticks in my mind. We'd been up late one night, drinking hooch, and the guys in the cell upstairs were shouting at us to keep the noise down. There was a lot of verbal abuse shouted back and forth through the windows. The following day, three of them came down to our cell and got mouthy, acting like they wanted a fight.

Lee just sat there with his back to them making a roll up.. 'Come in' he said, licking the cigarette paper. 'And close the door.'

They were caught of guard.

Lee turned around in his seat and lit his roll up.

'You've left the door open' he explained calmly 'If we're going to have a little chat we should do it in private.'

They knew that there were screws just a few feet from our door and that they'd intervene before anything too serious happened. So he'd called their bluff.

'Close the door and we'll talk' repeated Lee, still sitting calmly and smoking.

They knew talking wasn't going to be on the agenda if they closed the door, and that it would take a while before the screws got in and helped them.

'We're not looking for trouble!' said their ringleader. What a change of attitude! I realised then how much front and bravado there was in prison. All these people giving it the big 'un actually crumbled if you fronted up to them. They want to look like big men but really just want an easy life. That was a useful lesson that served me well for the rest of my sentence.

* * *

Not long after we arrived at Camp Hill, Allen and Chris Carroll were arrested and stood trial. Poor Chris was actually arrested in France and served a couple of years in prison there. Upon his release he was met at the prison gates by the English police and taken into custody to stand trial in the UK.

As none of our initial group were going to give evidence at their trial, our stories of them being the criminal masterminds behind the whole enterprise never came up. And as we were all already convicted and sentenced they were able to point the finger of blame at us.

Ultimately they got sentences of a similar length to ours but our paths never crossed in prison.

* * *

It's amazing how much time you can spend with people inside and have no idea what they're in for. If someone in prison asked you what you're in for, you knew they were relatively new to the system. It's not an etiquette thing, you just got bored of hearing the same old things. GBH, robbery, armed robbery, dealing, theft, whatever. You just got bored of asking, so you wouldn't bother any more.

About five months after arriving at Camp Hill, everything changed. A wing at another prison, HMP Blundeston, had closed and a bunch of prisoners were being moved to Camp Hill, so some of us had to move out to make room. Both of the Lees were told they were going to be moved to another jail, HMP Coldingley. The same day they were moving, the fourth person in our cell, Kevin, had reached the end of his sentence and was being released.

Mr Jenkins, one of the screws, suggested that I might want to move into a different cell with other people I already knew rather than have three new cell mates.

'This new lot are a bad bunch' he warned.

I didn't have to think about it for long.

'No, I'm staying put' I insisted. The way I saw it, this was my cell, my home. These new guys would come in and they could do things my way.

Kevin was the first to go. The whole time he'd been our cellmate, we would wind him up, saying that we thought he was a sex offender.

'May God forgive you for your sins, Kevin, because no one else will' I joked as he packed up to go.

Then Lee and Smithy were told it was time for them to head over to the prison reception for their transfer.

'Look after yourself mate. I'll write to you when I get there' said Lee. And then they were gone.

I had a couple of hours to myself waiting for my new cell mates. Had I made a mistake? I started to worry that maybe I should have moved to another cell. Then I started trying to work out who I might have pissed off and should watch out for now I didn't have Lee and Smithy with me. I snapped out of it when I heard the jangle of keys and my cell door opened.

In walked my new cell mates. One was a Scottish guy and I couldn't understand a word he said. The other was a Yardie and the third, a guy from south London. They all knew each other well from the previous prison. I knew now what it felt like to be the fourth man in the cell, the odd one out. I lasted about three hours before I asked to be moved to another cell.

'No hard feelings guys' I said 'But I'm going to leave you to it'.

Yeah, whatever' said one of them as he lay stretched out on Smithy's bed.

Chapter Ten

PART OF THE FURNITURE

'Well, you lasted about an hour more than I thought you would' Mr Jenkins smirked as I moved my stuff into the cell next door with Lee Parker and Neil Higgins. I knew them both as they'd been neighbours for a while and I was much more comfortable as soon as I moved in. There had been two empty beds in their cell due to all the moving around. The other space was filled by a new guy, Bob Thomas.

I instantly liked Bob. A black guy in his late 30s or early 40s. He was a good friend of another guy on the wing called Roger Greenman, who I also knew. Just like a Mr Baker ends up making cakes, Roger ended up selling weed in large quantities and everyone just called him "Green Man".

Parker was quite a character. He fancied himself as a bit of an intellectual and he was always very nice and polite to everyone. If he wasn't in front of the mirror checking that his shoulder-length hair looked perfect then he was wandering about the cell in a dressing gown he'd somehow managed to get his hands on.

One night, a few weeks after I moved into the cell, we were all sat around a coffee table (another item Parker had managed to acquire) watching a TV documentary about the roots of civilisation. It was about 9pm and our latest batch of hooch was being shared out so we were getting a bit drunk. Lee was eating a bowl of cornflakes and was discussing the programme with Bob and it started to get a little heated on the topic of race.

'Can we just chill the fuck out and watch the telly?' I asked. Parker was not listening. Instead he said to Bob 'My people were wiping their arse with silk while your people were still in the trees'.

Before he even finished the sentence, Bob leant forward and whacked the bowl of cornflakes out of his hands, spilling them all over his dressing gown. Both Neil and I jumped up to try to diffuse the situation but the alcohol had got the better of Parker. 'My cornflakes! You bastard, I'll fucking have you now' he screamed.

Bob just laughed. I think he struggled to take seriously the long-haired guy in front of him with cornflakes and milk all over his dressing gown. But Parker was adamant - he wanted a fight. So Neil and I climbed to one of the top bunks and let them get on with it, with us having ringside seats.

Bob stood there with his fists raised like a professional boxer. Lee copied him and for a few minutes they just circled each other. Parker tried to throw a few jabs but nothing connected. Then Bob let loose a series of perfect punches that splattered blood around the walls of the cell.

Eventually Parker realised he hadn't got a chance and threw in the towel. He shook Bob's hands. 'Yeah, good fight mate. You've got a mean left hook on you. Well done'. His nose was spread across his face but he was still being polite about it.

We agreed not to tell anyone outside of the cell what had gone on. We did not want their respective mates getting involved and stirring things up again. But in the morning, the state of Parker's face meant there was no hiding what had happened. Once word spread, I started getting a load of grief for "not sticking up for the white man".

* * *

The highlight of the week in prison was "Canteen" on Friday evenings. If you had money sent in you could have about £10 a week to spend.

Added to that were any wages you'd earned, which could be anything from £7.50 to £20. You ordered what you wanted by ticking boxes on a form. There was a fairly wide selection, from tobacco and phone cards to chocolate and even packets of noodles. You handed in the form and a week later, you'd collect your order, or canteen.

For security reasons, your order was in a heat-sealed transparent bag so there was no chance of anyone stealing it or of getting any contraband smuggled in via the external company that organised the canteen.

The screws opened the cells a few at a time for inmates to go downstairs to collect their stuff. As the orderlies were left unlocked, they were usually found hanging around downstairs while everyone collected their goodies.

One of the orderlies, a big guy called Darren, serving a long sentence for robbing other drug dealers, ran the laundry. He came to my cell one Friday and said 'Jacko, sort us a packet of noodles' I told him I didn't have any. 'Yes you do' he smiled. 'You've got three chicken and two beef. A chicken one will do'.

I quickly realised that the transparent bags and the orderlies seeing everything meant he knew exactly who had what. 'Fuck off and buy your own' I said. Just like I'd learned from Lee - it's all bravado. You front them out and they back down.

'You sure about that?' he asked. 'Yeah, sod off' I said. He laughed and walked out. It was all light hearted but it felt weird. Like he knew something I didn't.

The next morning I went to the wing laundry to pick up my clothes. As usual, all my clothes other than what I was wearing were in there.

'It's not ready yet' Darren told me. 'Come back later.'

So I did. And it still was not ready.

I realised I was being punished for not handing over the noodles Darren wanted. This childish farce went on for three days while I was left wearing the same clothes, which by now were beginning to hum.

He was twice my size and width but what other choice did I have? Somehow I built up the bottle to go and have it out with him. I found him in the laundry and demanded my gear. I tried to get right in his face, which was a bit hard given his height. He thought it was hilarious and creased up laughing. But I got my bag of laundry without any trouble.

The following Friday after canteen Darren turned up at my cell again.

'All right Jacko? Sort us out a packet of noodles mate?' he said with a smirk.

'Sure, chicken or beef?'

* * *

I was still teaching at the education department under the watchful eye of Ian. But he was taking days off sick more and more frequently so I was occasionally left to take the class on my own. Meanwhile, one of the other courses on offer was cooking. Everyone wanted to do it because you could get freshly cooked food that was a million times better than the junk served up on the wings. I became effective at working out when the class was being held and would drop in to get some freshly fried chips.

The screws had come to trust me, so when a vacancy came up for a new orderly to take on the job of wing painter, I was given it. My new improved status gave me a two-man cell. I enjoyed the privilege of our doors being open during the day so that we could have our showers and play pool, after cleaning the wing and painting. I relished this freedom as well being able to go to the library more often. I'd just ask the screws to unlock the wing and I had access to as many books as I wanted.

You'd think that being the wing painter I'd have to do a fair bit of painting. Well, you'd be wrong.

All the guys in prison, without exception, took real pride in their cells. I guess it was because it was the one thing which they had control over in their lives inside. Most of the cells were incredibly clean and tidy. People would be really competitive over who had the shiniest floor. And, of course, if they wanted their cell to look nice, it was going to need a lick of paint every now and then. So they'd ask me, the wing painter, to paint if for them.

'Sure, I'll put in on my list. I'll probably get around to it by Easter' was my usual response.

'Easter? It's mid-July and I'm going home in January!'

They're locked in a cell with nothing to do most of the day, so I knew they would rather paint it themselves if I gave them the materials. But I'd complain 'I can't do that, I'd lose my job' when they asked, unless that is an ounce of tobacco was forthcoming for paint and brushes. The cellmates had a fun day painting before I came to collect the paint. I'd get the credit for it from the screws, plus my tobacco from inmates, who were pleased with their freshly-painted home. It was a win-win situation and everyone was happy!

Like many of the shenanigans inside, the screws knew exactly what was going on but turned a blind eye to it.

I was getting very settled and comfortable. As usual, the screws would open the cells at 8am to get everyone up. I'd stay in bed and occasionally someone who'd just been kicked out of their own pit by a screw would say 'What about Jacko? How comes he gets away with it?'. 'Don't you worry about Jacko' they'd respond. I was getting all the perks of being an orderly and I filled my afternoons teaching at the education department. I was on to a good thing.

Thanks to my friends at interFACE, I built up an incredible collection of more than 200 music cassettes, which I painstakingly colour-coded for genre, each with their own catalogue number. I started lending them out - not for a charge but in return for favours, which put me in good standing. The screws got a bit annoyed as there was always a queue at my door when they were trying to lock us up at night. People called my cell "Red Records" after a well known shop in Brixton.

There were still a lot of drugs around. Unfortunately, the system drove people to heroin instead of "softer" drugs like cannabis. Heroin is only detectable in the system for 24 hours after you've taken it, whereas cannabis stays around for two weeks. So, given the random drug testing, it was safer to take heroin than cannabis.

If you failed a drug test it could mean being transferred to a harsher wing or even additional sentence time. But the screws wanted to show good numbers in their reports to demonstrate that the drug-free wing was having an impact on reducing drug use. So if you were selected for a random drug test the screws would usually make sure you knew about it 10 minutes beforehand. That meant that getting your hands on someone's urine you knew was clean could put you in the clear. Everyone knew I never took drugs, so they quite literally took the piss out of me. My urine became incredibly valuable on testing days. I could easily make more in cards and tobacco out of my pee than I could possibly buy in an entire month. This caused a problem for me as there's only a certain amount of tobacco and phone cards you're allowed to have at any one time. So I started lending tobacco to others. This didn't help much as I'd then get double back - double bubble! But it meant I was a popular guy on the wing.

You'd occasionally get a guy that would borrow from you and not pay you back. For me, it wasn't worth the hassle trying to chase the debt. As far as I was concerned I'd gladly write of the half ounce of tobacco and never ever ever lend to you again. It was a system that seemed to work. People paid me back because they knew they'd need my services again.

* * *

One Thursday afternoon I was waiting to be locked up after lunch. I was with my cellmate, Eddie West, and another orderly called Dodger, who looked like a Dickensian scoundrel, feral in appearance and well-known throughout the prison system. Dodger is one of those guys that has spent more of his adult life in prison than outside of it.

As it was the day before canteen, everyone was running low on tobacco and I had lent out a lot. A guy called Flex, from a four-man cell upstairs, came in. He was a double for Manchester United and England footballer Rio Ferdinand. He was always asking to borrow "a bit of tobacco". He never actually took a full half-ounce packet because he'd need to give it back to me. He asked again and I said no. He kept pleading, and after the third time I'd had enough and told him to fuck off.

He lunged at me, but before he did any damage, Darren - who still ran the laundry - grabbed him. Flex screamed and shouted he would kill me, kicking out, hurtling the coffee table, a parting gift from Parker, across the room and slicing into Ed's leg.

'You can't hit Jacko' said Dodger 'That's like hitting a part of the furniture!'
Flex was dragged away, yelling threats at me, saying that as soon as they open the cells at 2.30 he'd be coming for me.

I spent the next two hours worrying about what he might do to me. Was I just supposed to sit there and wait for the beating? I banged on the wall of the cell next door to talk to my neighbour, Green Man. He had a solid metal bar and, responding to my plea, he managed to pass it to me through the windows of our cells.

Would I really use it? I slipped the bar up my sleeve. The adrenalin had been building up for two hours while I paced my cell. As soon as the door opened at 2.30, I stormed up the stairs and burst into Flex's cell. I shook the bar from my sleeve but just as I was about to confront him, he ran at me and threw his arms around me. He hugged me and apologised. While I'd been working myself up into a frenzy, he'd been thinking what an idiot he was. We fell about laughing and I was massively relieved.

I had learned very quickly that one of the dangers of prison life was just how quickly the most simple things, taken the wrong way, could turn violent. It was always one of my biggest worries. You could end up in a position where you had to attack to defend yourself. If things escalated, you might kill someone and spend the rest of your life in prison.

* * *

Every Saturday you had the prison equivalent of a fry-up for dinner. If you said you were vegan a slightly different menu, including mushrooms, was available. Vegans were given four mushrooms with their meal. If the kitchen was told we had 10 vegans on the wing then we would get 40 mushrooms sent for serving. I like mushrooms. Forty came over, 10 were put aside for me. No-one had ever complained. Everyone knew this was the way it was. Even when the screws occasionally helped sort out the food the first thing they did was to put my mushrooms to one side for me.

One Saturday the senior officer on duty was Miss Pratt, a horrible little woman. Someone found out they were getting less mushrooms than they should and complained. She checked with the kitchen and deduced that someone was stealing food. All six of us orderlies got a bollocking. And we were all threatened with losing our jobs. It was a big deal. Later on, whenever it was talked about it was referred to as Mushroomgate.

We couldn't bear the thought of not being orderlies with our privileged positions and going back to the daily grind of an ordinary prisoner, having to queue for phones, showers and the pool table. I had to cut down on my mushroom habit. Word circulated and many of the guys would give me their mushrooms. It was a ridiculous situation to be in. But the main reason that episode has stuck with me is because I remember thinking 'How can I be in a position where this horrible woman has such control on my life?'. It really highlighted for me what a complete loss of liberty means.

* * *

On a rare occasion when I did get to paint, I was re-coating a door frame, and a fellow prisoner said a plane had crashed into the World Trade Center.

I went down to the TV room at the end of the wing to watch it and could not believe the ignorance of those who were laughing at the scenes unfolding in New York. I think they couldn't relate to it as being real-life. But I had been to New York and even contemplated living there. While I had been out on bail and having dinner with Nancy, Lucy and their mother Joey, I took a phone call from an employment agency asking if I was interested in an IT job based in one of the Twin Towers. A shiver went down my spine. I could have been in that building. Going to prison could have saved my life. I was shocked.

As it became apparent that it was extremists, virtually all of the Muslim prisoners were suddenly terrified they would be moved to high security prisons. Ironically, that included yours truly, as long before, I had ticked the box to say I was Muslim because I was tipped off that they were given better food during Ramadan.

* * *

Ian's increased absences in the education department were explained soon after. He had ME and was often off sick for days. I would take over running the classes. The screws knew I was teaching and that news had reached the governor and even the prison authorities. I was awarded a Millennium Volunteers certificate signed by David Blunkett, then Home Secretary, for this voluntary work - the first inmate in the country to receive one. It was casually handed over to me by the head of the education department one afternoon in the corridor. I was really proud of this, despite the lack of ceremony.

My parole was due on December 9, 2002, two and a half years into my sentence. My voluntary teaching work was always going to stand me in good stead to secure early release but I felt this would seal the deal.

* * *

Prison is often seen as a harsh place and it is. But you also get to see some of the better side of human nature. There was a guy in one of the cells upstairs. I don't remember his real name but everyone called him Billy Elliot because of his diminutive build and slightly effeminate nature. He pretty much kept himself to himself. But it was apparent that he was getting picked on by another inmate called Delroy, and it was escalating. Delroy was your typical bully - going after those he thought were weak and vulnerable.

One week, Delroy decided to rob Billy of his entire canteen. None of the orderlies had any particular attachment to Billy but we all thought it was not on. We decided we needed to put a stop to it. Darren, the head orderly, got a group of us together and paid Delroy a visit in his cell. He was told in no uncertain terms that if he bothered Billy again he'd have to answer to us. Billy was left alone and finished his sentence in peace.

* * *

When an orderly vacancy came up, I tried to make sure someone I knew got it. There was a guy called Simon, a cellmate of Flex who seemed OK and fortunately he got the job and became my cellmate. We got on really well and became good friends. He was 10 years older than me and we'd have quite in-depth conversations. We played a lot of chess together too. He would almost invariably win. I've beaten him twice in the 15 years I have known him inside and outside of prison. I credit those matches for keeping me sane while I was banged up, or at least stopping my brain from turning to mush. There wasn't much intellectual stimulation to be had.

One of his ex-cellmates was a guy called Lee Budd. He was on the phone during association and was on it for quite a while, thanks to the shaven phonecards he had. A queue started to form and people were getting annoyed with him.

'Hold on, I am talking to my mum' he said.

'Well, just hurry up!' yelled someone else.

Lee turned round and smashed the poor guy around the head with the phone. He had blood spurting out of his head. Lee thought it might be wise to flee the scene, so he headed up to my cell where Simon and I were playing chess. He told us what happened and then went quiet and thoughtful for a moment:

'Maybe I should do that anger management course.' he said.

Say what you like about Lee Budd, he was certainly self aware!

* * *

After a while you almost forget the outside world exists. You are totally shut off from society. The prison itself is your own little world and other wings are like neighbouring towns from which you hear stories about incidents and new arrivals. In a way, it makes it easier to do your sentence with little outside contact. You're not reminded of what you're missing and can create your own reality within the prison walls.

We all had cardboard panels next to our beds and it was customary to stick up photos, using toothpaste as glue. I felt sorry for those who had pictures of their children pinned up. I could understand why inmates with kids chose not to have their pictures there to remind them every day of what they were missing. It was hard enough to do time away from your friends. I couldn't imagine what it must be like to be away from your children for a long period of time.

Besides letters and photos, visits were the other way of staying in touch. You'd get issued two Visiting Orders (VOs) each month. But the Isle of Wight was a pain in the arse for visitors to get to, so not everyone used their VOs. I was told not to expect any visits or letters from male friends. I thought, 'My mates will. They'll be here'. But apart from Ben, I didn't have one male visitor and very rarely did I get any letters from male friends. Thankfully, I had lots of female friends though. Lin and Elise, two girls I'd known from interFACE kept in touch with me throughout my entire sentence. They'd write just about every week and rarely a month would go by without them visiting me.

* * *

By now, Ian, had been totally signed off sick and I was running the IT classes full-time.

Mr. Jenkins, one of the screws on our wing, stopped me one day.

'Jacko, why aren't you in an open prison yet?' he asked me.

I told him I thought it was a bloody good question.

'I keep putting in my applications but I don't get a response'

'You really don't understand, do you?' He asked.
I was intrigued. I didn't have a clue why I hadn't been transferred.

'You are teaching in the education department. If you stop, they would have to employ a teacher on around £30,000, which would be out of their budget. If you want to go to an open prison, stop bloody teaching!'

With that he walked off and I was left to think about what he had said. The penny dropped.

The same day, I handed in my notice, saying I didn't want to teach any more. No-one had any complaints and I stopped there and then. Within a couple of weeks I was told I had been reclassified as a "Category D" prisoner and would be be transferred to Ford.

I was over the moon. It is the Promised Land. HMP Butlins. I had six months of my sentence left.

On the day of my transfer, I was in a holding cell at the front of the prison and it dawned on me that this was the last time I was going to be locked in a cell. A smile came over my face. I was on the home run.

Category D prisoners are given a certain amount of trust and I was allowed to make my own way to HMP Ford in West Sussex, using a travel grant. I was told to arrive by 4pm. I had a passing thought to go AWOL but dismissed it very quickly.

Ben picked me up in his BMW convertible. It was a summer day and the roof was down. I shouted at him to slow down as I thought he was doing 100mph but, in fact, he was only going at 25. For the last 18 months nothing had gone faster than a quick walk.

On the ferry leaving the Isle of Wight, I realised that, bizarrely, I was actually quite sad to be transferring. I had a cushy number and good friends. I was part of the furniture and a character. I would get my morning lie-in and I was settled. Did I really want to be leaving? I guess I was on the verge of being institutionalised.

Even now when I think back to my time at Camp Hill, I miss it a little bit.

Chapter Eleven

KEEP OFF THE GRASS

HMP Ford seemed like an idyllic village with its manicured cricket pitch, tidy flower beds, "Keep off the grass" signs and prisoners strolling around like it was a Sunday afternoon.

Ben dropped me off and I knew I only had six months to go on my sentence. It was summertime and that's what made the mood even more casual.

I checked in as if I was going into a hotel for six months but as with any prison there would be the inevitable induction process of filling out forms and being told the rules. I was one of 20 new guests, sorry, inmates, who had arrived at the same time, and we were all sent to a large dormitory. The atmosphere was very relaxed compared to the other prisons I'd been in. But hanging over you was the constant threat that if you broke any of the rules, you'd be sent back to a closed prison in the blink of an eye. Even the "Keep off the grass" signs were strictly obeyed.

Ford had an odd mix of inmates. There were lifers finishing long sentences for murder, armed robbers coming to the end of 12-year sentences and many first-time offenders, mostly in for relatively minor offences, including driving-related charges or theft. Then there were the white collar criminals - the fraudsters. And finally you had bent former police officers and solicitors.

I fell in with a small group straight away, a real mixed bag of people. An American guy called Valentine Brown who was inside for handling stolen property, including, rather bizarrely, horse saddles. A mixed race guy, about five years older than me, he knew how to work the system and bet me he could get transferred from the dormitory to a one-man cell the same day. No chance! I took the bet. Within an hour he was packing his things having just been given his own cell in a prime location.

I went to see him that evening to pay the bet - a half ounce of tobacco - and he revealed his secret. He'd gone to the screws and started crying, pleading for a cell of his own because he had been raped in an American prison and was terrified of it happening again if he stayed in the dormitory. They took pity on the poor shaking wreck in front of them and immediately granted his request. None of it was true, of course, but he knew that because he claimed it happened in the States, they couldn't check.

Another of the group was Dave, an overweight Worzel Gummidge lookalike. Then there was Titch and Trevor, who were joined at the hip. Titch was a young guy in for the first time, while Trevor was an old hand at prison. He wore glasses with ridiculously thick lenses and spent his time making amazingly intricate model horse carriages out of matchsticks. Finally, there was Roddy, an ex-magistrate and former chairman of Boodles, one of the oldest private members' clubs in London. He had the poshest accent I'd ever heard.

Those of us without Valentine's brass balls were on the dormitory for a couple of days before getting our permanent quarters. We had to fill in forms to say where in the prison we wanted to work and I opted for the education department. Within days I was assigned to be a receptionist there, with the official title "educational orderly". I was given my own room on Block M3, one of about a dozen eight-room huts. They were all single rooms and each hut had its own showers and telephone. The door to the hut itself was never locked and we all had our own room key.

Each night at about 9pm, the screws would come into the hut and shout

'By your doors!'. We then had to all stand by our doors to be counted. It was their way of making sure no-one had done a runner. On my first night in the hut, after the headcount, it started to rain really heavily. I went and stood near the open door and got soaked. It felt amazing to be able to do that after two years of being locked up every night.

Although the extra freedom was great, I was missing Camp Hill a little. I had my set routines there. I had my friends and I had become very settled. I had all the privileges I could get. I was well-known and had a certain standing within the prison community. But here at Ford.I was just another faceless number

I quickly established good terms with the two women who, as senior administrators, ran the education unit - Charlotte and Clare. The unit was open five days a week, nine to five, and there was a whole range of courses from basic IT to money management. I ran the reception desk along with another orderly, Bob. He was an ex-police officer and his appearance and demeanour reminded me of Father Christmas.

I soon fell into a routine, a part of which was mealtimes, of course, and very different to Camp Hill. There it had been very regimented and after getting the food you were locked up in the cell to eat. Here there was an open canteen and we had a two-hour period in which to have lunch and eat it on trestle tables.

I would meet up with Valentine or others from our group and we would go for lunch together. On the way to the canteen we would stroll past the prison Post Office to see if our names were on the list for those with post to collect. We usually went just after the rush of prisoners. But we didn't leave it too late because you would end up with soggy chips and food that had been sitting around for too long.

The educational unit tended to quieten down towards the end of the day, so I got Ben to send in Visual Studio - some computer software for programmers. I installed it on one of the computers so that I could practise my programming.

Evenings were very laid back. I would stroll around with Roddy and we would stop and chat with friends, who would often be strolling in the other direction around the inside of the perimeter fence. Roddy seemed to know everyone in the prison, and there were some interesting characters.

Amongst Roddy's pals was Jonathan Barnham, ex-fiancée of former *EastEnders* actress Martine McCutcheon. He was serving time for his part in a cannabis importation plot.

Also at Ford at that time was Jonathan Rees. His name came up a lot in the News of The World hacking scandal years later. He'd also been allegedly involved with the axe murder of his former business partner in the 80's, he was never convicted though. He was serving time for another offence.

Another character was David Shayler. He'd worked for MI5 and had been convicted for breaking the Official Secrets Act by passing information to the Mail on Sunday. David was convinced he was going to be attacked and had paid two big guys to act as his bodyguards in the prison. It was wasted money as no one knew or cared who he was.

You sure got a different class of criminal at Ford!

Late one evening I was sitting in my room reading a book when my neighbour, Arthur, knocked on my door and invited me into his room for cheese and biscuits. I thought he was joking and that it was going to be the prison equivalent. But he had prepared a veritable feast with

Jacob's cream crackers, a slab of cheese and a bottle of vodka, which he had just gone and bought from Tesco! If you were willing to take the risk, and many were, then you could jump the prison fence, go to the shops and get back before anyone knew you were gone.

My neighbour on the other side of me was Neville, who in his teens had killed his mum and was finishing a life sentence. We got on really well. He was not much older than me.

Also in my hut was Chris, a Greek guy finishing a long sentence for armed robbery. He spent most of his time in the gym and had probably spent the best part of his 12-year sentence working out in gyms in one prison or another around the country. But his problem was that he only worked on his top half. He had huge arms and an extremely broad chest but spindly little legs which looked as if they could barely support him.

He wore a gold chain with a gold shotgun and he would break open the barrel and inside were two little gold cartridges. He was very proud of it and it was round his neck all the time.

I never really used the gym much myself. On one Sunday afternoon at Ford, a bunch of us were strolling around feeling a bit bored. We noticed the gym was empty and there were four rowing machines sitting there unused. So we decided to have a competition to see who could row 5km the fastest. I won, but nearly killed myself in the process. I went back to my cell and I slept for two days.

* * *

There are a whole bunch of prisoners who work outside the prison in the community resettlement programme. They are prisoners coming to the end of sentences and are gradually being acclimatised to being back in society. They have their own routine and are housed in their own units at the other side of the prison near the dining halls. You tended not to see them during the day because they were away working.

One day I was in the lunch queue and I saw one of the guys who worked outside and he was reading a book on computer programming. I told him we had the software in the education department for that particular programming language. He was surprised. But we arranged to meet later that evening. He was only just learning about programming and I showed him how to use it.

Steve explained how the resettlement programme worked: You had to work six weeks voluntarily unpaid and after that you agree with the employer an hourly rate if they want to keep you on. He was working in the accounts department of a company called Farplants, the sales arm of a collective of independent nurseries. He was trying to write a programme to make his job easier. He currently had to go through a laborious process of regularly checking if there were any new files in the sales folder. He wanted something that would watch the folder and let him know as soon as a file arrived.

I told him I could write something that does that in about an hour. He challenged me, and not one to shy away from a challenge, I wrote it there and then with him. I called it CarefulEye. I saved it on to a disc and he took it in to work the next day. He was so impressed that the next evening he handed me a 50 gram pouch of tobacco. He asked me to let him know when I was able to go on the programme. He thought he could wangle me a job with him. And that's exactly what happened.

As soon as I was eligible for the work scheme, I went to see the officer in charge and asked if I could join the scheme. He confirmed I was eligible but would have to wait for a job to come up. I said 'Well, actually, I have one'.

I got onto the scheme and went to work with Steve. It was a mile from the prison and we would cycle there and back on prison bikes. We would leave the office half an hour early and as Steve was being paid we would stop off for a kebab in the village on our way back to prison.

The IT systems within the company were old and there was a lot of work for me updating them. There was lots to keep me busy. Steve and I shared an office with Tim who worked as a trainee in the accounts department but was also interested in learning about programming. It wasn't long before the pair of them had sussed me out. Tim pointed out that I always confidently say I could do anything that was asked of me, and then use search engines to find out how to actually do it. Yep, that's exactly how I worked!

I reached the end of my voluntary free six-week period and I had to sit down with Vernon, the IT director, to discuss a paid position. It was a given that I was going to get one. It was just how much they were going to pay me. He said 'You are going to be very pleased that we are going to pay you more than we have ever paid anyone before. We are going to pay you £7 an hour'.

I knew I was in a good position. They were seeing immediate benefits, which improved the business, and they'd have had to pay a lot more on the open market to get someone to do what I was doing. I told Vernon that I only had three months left on my sentence and I was seriously considering just relaxing for 3 months and not working at all. If he wanted to convince me to stay and work for him then he would have to double what was on the table.

He realised I wasn't going to be taken advantage of and eventually agreed on £13 an hour. I'd won my first business negotiation! Vernon duly filled in the form with my hourly rate, which I then had to give back to the officer in charge of the resettlement work programme back at Ford.

I handed him the form and began to walk away he called me back

'Jackson. Is this right? £13 an hour?' He looked at me and told me to sit down. 'We have a bit of problem here'

I didn't understand.

'You're getting paid more than I am. More than any of my colleagues are' he explained. 'I'm happy to see you do well, but others might not be. so don't let anyone know how much you're getting paid or they might mess it up for you out of envy'

* * *

I fell into my new routine for the final stage of my sentence. I went to work with Steve in the morning, and then in the evenings I'd chill out with Roddy and the others, walking around the prison chatting with friends. Every other weekend I would alternate between a prison visit and a day release when a friend would come and sign me out for a few hours. As a middle ground between being locked up in prison and being a free man, it worked. I certainly felt more able to be a part of the wider world than I did after my time at Camp Hill.

One morning I was walking past reception when I heard someone yell out 'Oi, Jacko!'. It took me totally by surprise as no-one had called me that since Camp Hill. But there, larger than life, was my old cellmate and chess tutor, Simon.

He had just been transferred and knew I was here. He fell into our group. Roddy, Simon and I all had similar release dates. In hindsight it would appear that that's how the friendships were formed. It makes sense, you wouldn't want to spend too much time with someone who is out months or even years before you - it'd drive you potty.

Walking to lunch with Simon a few days later, we stopped off at the Post Office as usual to see if we had any mail. My name and number was on the list of people who had mail to collect. It was nothing unusual as I used to getting occasional post from friends, particularly my mates at interFACE and from Joey - Nancy and Lucy's mum.

But on this occasion I was in for a bit of a surprise. There was one letter with handwriting that I did not recognise. I opened it and it started *'You probably don't remember me'*. It was from Nadia. I was so excited. I read the letter five times and I didn't even make it to the dinner hall. I just sat down and was reading it over and over again and went straight to my room to write back.

Simon knew who she was because I had spoken a lot about her at Camp Hill. She had started working in recruitment in Essex and across her desk came a CV from a girl called Katie who we had both known when we were younger. She immediately phoned Katie for a chat and they started reminiscing about all the old faces. My name came up and Katie said 'Didn't you hear? He is doing time' Katie told her what had happened. Nadia was shocked, but she did a deal with Katie: you get me his address and I'll get you a job.

I wrote back and then Nadia said she wanted to come to visit me. It was the first time I had seen her in close to 10 years but she was still as beautiful as ever with her dark curly hair. We immediately clicked and it was as if the intervening years had not happened. She had been in a relationship with another guy, who actually drove her to the prison to see me.

It was arranged for her to take me out for a few hours on one of the days I was allowed out of prison as part of the resettlement programme. We spent the day together and hit it off quite quickly. We started writing letters all the time and talking on the phone. I knew in my heart I was falling in love - it helped that it was late in my sentence and I just had three more months to serve. Every opportunity I had to spend time outside of the prison was spent with her.

Nadia felt exactly the same way and we shared our feelings as we talked about making a life together on my release. Then, on one visit, she dropped a bombshell. She was pregnant. She'd conceived the first time we were together. There were mixed emotions on both sides. We were ecstatically happy. But Nadia was under a lot of pressure from her family not to get involved with someone who had been in prison and certainly not to have a baby with them.

I knew I wanted to be with Nadia and have children with her. It was just the timing.
We discussed it a lot. After a lot of talk and soul-searching we decided to go ahead and she would have the baby. It gave us both something to look forward too.

* * *

With a baby on the way I realised I needed to work out a plan for what I was going to do on my release. It wasn't just me I had to support. I would have a partner and a baby. My mind went back to the guys at Camp Hill locked away from their kids. There's no way I was going to risk being like that. Together with my three closest friends, Steve, Simon and Roddy, my future was discussed at length. Over and over again. In prison, the one thing of which we had a seemingly never-ending supply of was time.

I now had to decide what I was going to do on the outside. I of course had my 20% of Ben's company to look forward to. I discussed the situation with Roddy. I'd explained that Ben had bailed me out in the United States and I had worked for him for a year, but it was Roddy's opinion that I was the one who had been taken advantage of because I had not been paid properly at all whilst on bail.

'But Ben has given me 20 per cent of the company instead' I explained. 'Do you have the Share Certificates?' he asked.

I didn't know what they were, but I told him I had the contract I signed back in my cell. He suggested I went and found it. So I ran off to my cell to get the paperwork. When I got back to Roddy's room he had one of his many friends with him. The friend was a solicitor before he'd got into whatever trouble had landed him in jail.

I waited anxiously while he read it thoroughly. He gave it back to me and said it was not worth the paper it was written on, explaining in no uncertain terms that I certainly did not own 20 per cent of Ben's company. What it did say was that I could possibly own 20 per cent of the company in the future but it was so one-sided in favour of Ben it was not worth having.

'My dear boy' said Roddy in his Etonian accent, 'You really must resolve this before your release. You have responsibilities now.'

In my mind, I had been going back to work with Ben and we had been in touch the whole time I had been at Ford. Thanks to the software in the education department and internet access at Farplants, I'd increased the amount of work I'd been doing for him. He'd occasionally send in £20 to keep my funds topped up. I was sure we'd get this situation sorted in no time.

I emailed Ben from work and told him what I had learned about the contract and asked what he suggested we do. He said I was right but he had been made to do it that way by his solicitors. I told him I could not work for him on that basis. He was obviously worried about losing my expertise and instantly replied that he would get it sorted straight away so that I actually owned 20 percent of the company.

As the weeks passed, needing that certainty, I kept pestering him for confirmation that it had now been arranged as we had agreed. It became apparent that it wasn't going to happen and Ben was not going to be forthcoming with any permanent deal. I felt stuck.

That evening, walking around the prison as usual, I spotted a poster at the Education Department. It was advertising a talk that was due to be given by the Prince's Trust. It was to explain the services they offered to help people when they finish their sentences, specifically around self employment.

About a dozen of us turned up and I was intrigued to learn about how they could help us to start our own businesses on release. It was something that had simply not occurred to me. In my head, people who started their own businesses had gone to Oxford or Cambridge. Not from my neck of the woods. But the more I thought about it, the more it made sense. I thought about what I had done with Ben and that surely I could find my own customers to do work for? I knew starting and running a business was probably far more complicated than that, but the Princes Trust said they'd give us all the help we needed to get started.

They said grants were available and, equally important, training and mentoring. Before I'd even left the room, I'd decided I was going to go for it.

The very next day I started on a business plan. I emailed Ben and politely told him not to worry about the 20 per cent as I was going to be doing my own thing when I got out. I wasn't expecting to hear back from him very quickly, he'd been incredibly slow to reply when I was chasing him for the new shares contract. But his reply was as instant as it was short. Just one line *"et tu Brute?"*

I had to Google the expression to find out what it meant - no surprise to Steve and Tim - but I didn't feel in any way that I had betrayed him. Ben came to see me and tried his hardest to talk me out of it. He told me how hard and complicated it was to run a business and said I would fail and would end up with nowhere to live and that I would be knocking on his door.

'It's the last thing you should be considering with a baby on the way.'

But my mind was made up and there was no changing it. The more he was telling me I shouldn't do it - couldn't do it - the more determined I was to make it a reality. I was going to set myself up as a programmer for hire, a freelance web developer. I felt my services would be in demand and my success with Farplants spurred me on - there must be similar companies where I could go in and make a difference.

* * *

My final two months at Ford seemed to go really quickly. I was working every day outside the prison and working on a business plan the rest of the time. Every other weekend I would get to see Nadia. She had her hands full trying to find us somewhere to stay temporarily when I was released.

A couple of weeks before my release I was allowed out for a whole weekend as a part of the resettlement programme. Nadia's cousin, Christian, let us stay with him and his family for the weekend but it was over very quickly.

Towards the end of a prison sentence they say you are "gate happy" as you prepare for your new life on the outside, on the other side of the prison gate.

And the day before you are released there is a whole load of paperwork to do where you go round getting each department to sign you off in what is known as the "paper chase".

As I am chasing round the prison I think back to my flannel in Clayton. I suspect the paper chase isn't really necessary but I think the authorities get you to do it so you are not climbing the walls.

December 9 was to be the day of my release just as I'd calculated in the prison van two-and-a-half years ago. I said goodbye to my friends and promised to keep in touch. It helped that most of them were also due for release very soon. Joey picked me up in a taxi with Lucy and Nancy, whilst Nadia was getting our new home sorted. I'd saved a few thousand pounds from my work at Farplants and Nadia had found an inexpensive one-bedroom flat in Chadwell Heath that was to be our home.

The flat was tiny, but it was all we needed It had a bedroom, sitting room and a corner kitchen. What wasn't immediately obvious were the damp problems, or the millions of fleas living in the carpet. But it was home, and a damn sight better than where I had been. And the main thing was, I was with Nadia.

I thought that the resettlement programme at Ford - working outside the prison, occasional day release - had prepared me for being back in the real world and I wouldn't have any problems with adapting.

I remember going to the shop at the top of our road. I was standing there waiting for a gap in the traffic to cross the road. It wasn't a particularly busy road but there didn't seem to be an opportunity to cross because of all the fast moving traffic. A few other people managed to cross without any problems in the five minutes that I was stood there. I eventually got used to crossing roads again!

I was also very used to routine. When we had dinner and before I had finished I would want to know what was for dessert. Any cake would do, ideally with custard.

I got so much done in those first couple of weeks. I was like a whirlwind. I found my first few clients in the run up to Christmas. Ben needed me to do some work for him. I quoted him a much lower hourly rate than I was to everyone else, but he still thought I was charging too much. Reluctantly, he agreed.

The biggest help was a contract I agreed with Farplants, the company that had employed me at Ford. Some of the software I had written was now core to their business. One piece of software was called NITS, Nursery Information Transfer System, which would coordinate all their nurseries from the different sites back into head office. It was a vital piece of software and they couldn't take the risk that I would not be there if a problem arose. Tim had now moved from the accounts department and into IT. Tim and his manager agreed to pay me a £700 a month retainer to be on call for them. It was ideal for me, I had some guaranteed income and I would only have to go there if there was a problem that I couldn't deal with remotely.

But it wasn't all plain sailing and I still had some valuable lessons to learn. During my time in prison, I became friendly with a fellow inmate named Guy, who was serving a sentence for credit card fraud. On his release he was setting up a business called Versailles Beautiful Furniture. He needed a website and an e-commerce site. We agreed a price of £6,000. He'd been released just a couple of weeks before me and was keen to have everything up and running as soon as possible. So I pulled out all the stops and put in crazy hours to get it all done for him. I was proud of the work and excited for him to put it into practise. Guy said he loved it too, but he hadn't yet paid me a penny. He delayed his launch and kept coming up with excuses for why he hadn't paid me. Eventually he stopped taking my calls before doing a runner. I learned the valuable lesson of never doing work without getting paid something up front. It was a blow as I had made so many plans while in prison but I was still firing on all cylinders.

Suddenly I realised everyone was winding down for Christmas. And so did I.

Chapter Twelve

BUY A LOTTERY TICKET

No one would ever describe me as a romantic, but I knew Nadia was the one for me and I wanted to propose to her. I knew I would never be proposing to anyone else again in my life so I decided I really should make an effort.

Shortly before Christmas, I went out with my friend, Yomi, to buy an engagement ring. It wasn't so long ago that I'd ask him to ask Nadia if she'd go out with me at the swimming pool. Hopefully I'd get a more positive answer to the next question I was going to be asking her.

Once I'd bought the ring I went about disassembling a Christmas cracker. I carefully put the ring inside it. I wrote the words: "Will You Marry Me?" where the joke would have been. I had never been more serious in my life.

Christmas day came. It was just the two of us having a quiet Christmas lunch in the flat . When we pulled the cracker the ring flew across the floor and Nadia just caught a glimpse of the sparkle and asked where the other one was, thinking it was a pair of earrings. She certainly wasn't expecting an engagement ring and a proposal.

I picked up the ring and gave it to her and I felt she knew what was coming. I gave her the slip of paper to read and she started laughing nervously. I don't think she ended up saying "yes". She was overwhelmed and collapsed into nervous giggling. I made it clear I was serious and she obviously did accept.

* * *

I couldn't help thinking about my friends still inside - especially at Camp Hill, where December 25th is a day to forget. It is always quiet and subdued and inmates just want the hours to come and go quickly. I was pleased that I had come through my ordeal relatively unscathed. I'd learnt a lot of lessons whilst in prison. I realised I was there as a result of my own actions. It sounds obvious but I don't think a lot of people realise that they're responsible for their own lives.

I still see so many people I grew up with being blown about in the wind - ending up wherever their unplanned lives take them. I read somewhere that "if you don't have your own plan, you'll end up being a part of someone else's - and guess what they've got planned for you? Not much!" That resonated with me. I was determined to formulate my own plans and not bounce around at the mercy of the system, whether it was prison, welfare or society.

I don't mean to say that I now had a detailed plan for the rest of my life. But I did feel I had chosen a direction - to run my own business, be independent and provide (legally!) for my new family - and with that in mind I could take steps towards it. I knew that no one was going to do it for me and if I didn't succeed then I would not be able to blame any external factors. Wherever I end up in 10 years time will be as a result of what I do each year. What I do each year is made up of what I do each month, and what I do each month is made up of what I do each day, how hard I work and how I react to the challenges that would no doubt come up.

* * *

Money was still tight, whatever I was making from work was going on essentials. I was on a government "New Deal" scheme which meant I would still get benefits paid to me for 6 months while I tried to become self sufficient. But I was using an ancient computer Yomi had donated to me, and I was working from the corner of the front room. Literally on the floor in the corner. I didn't have a desk. I decided to contact the Prince's Trust as I thought there was good chance I'd be able to get a grant or a loan from them.

I filled in a form on their website where I outlined my plan for a business as a programmer-for-hire and explained I was looking for whatever help I could get.

Within a week I was set up to meet a business adviser who had been appointed to look after me - Heather Skea, to whom I presented my business plan at the Prince's Trust office in East London. I was genuinely expecting to get a pat on the head and a nice cheque for £5,000. It didn't quite go that way.

Heather went through the plan and pointed out some glaring holes. I had not done any forecasting on how much money I would make and no research on any competition that was out there. I was a bit taken aback. This wasn't what I was expecting. I didn't think they'd look too closely at my actual plan. I wasn't feeling too confident about what I'd written.

Whilst my prison buddies had been supportive about it, the only other person I'd shared any of my business idea with was Ben. But Heathers criticisms were valid and I never felt once from her that she was being judgemental or dismissing me or my plan - quite the opposite. Even at our first meeting I felt straight away that she was being incredibly supportive and her confidence in me filled me with confidence in myself.

It took the next two months to get the plan up to scratch, with lots of help from Heather. By March it was considered a strong enough proposal to go before the panel which approved grants. There were a group of about 12 of us, sitting at desks where we were quizzed one on one about our business plans and what we were going to do with the money if our grant applications were successful. That lasted about an hour and then the panel retired to make their decisions.

I knew I had a good chance of getting approved. I'd put a lot of work into the plan and I ticked all of the relevant boxes - care leaver, ex-con, no qualifications.

At the end of the day, I went home with the news that I had been approved for a grant of £1,500 and a low-interest loan of £2,500 - a huge amount of money!

.

Before they'd release the funds, I had to go on a one-day crash course in business management along with others that had recently been approved for funding. I sat next to a guy of about my age called Milton. He was starting as a web designer and had a great sense of humour. We immediately hit it off. . The course covered all sorts of things from bookkeeping to tax. A banker gave a workshop on opening a business account and there was a never-ending series of further workshops throughout the day. Although it was quite boring subject matter, it was useful information as it covered stuff I hadn't even considered before.

I can't say I was ever enamoured by the business side of things as I just wanted to get out there and start programming. Within days of the workshop I received the cash and was trading as Seventech Solutions. I went out and bought a computer, desk and business cards. I felt like I was rich.

There was a monthly Prince's Trust Event held at their offices in Moorgate for everyone who had recently received funding. The events were run by volunteers, headed up by an older gentleman called Ron

Roeder. Ron was a master of going around the room, spotting people on their own and introducing them to someone relevant. It was meant to be a networking event, but it was more of a peer support group. We were all from similar backgrounds and all determined to run our own businesses. I saw Milton there and we realised our skills were very complimentary. His clients wanted more than just a good-looking website, they wanted extra functionality of the type I could program. And while I could do all the techie side of building websites, I hadn't the foggiest idea on the design side and that's where he was in his element.

I attended the events every month. Milton and I would pick up a lot of business there but we'd also learn a lot. Ron would use his magical persuasive powers to get people to come and give talks for free. We'd typically have two 30 minutes talks each evening on different topics from time management, to doing your own PR, to selling to corporates. As an audience we were incredibly engaged so the speakers really enjoyed it too. Apart from the guy that was trying to sell us his "Millionaire Mindset" books. After relentless questioning from the audience, he finally conceded that he wasn't in fact a millionaire himself. The poor (no pun intended) guy couldn't wait to get out of there.

The talks were followed by drinks, sandwiches and networking. The format worked really well and lots of strong friendships and business relationships were formed.

Sometime later, there were some big staff changes at the Trust. Ron left and the events stopped. I ended up running them independently for a year or so under the name TrustNetworkers. I didn't have the same talents as Ron.

I remember asking a well known speaker to come and talk to the group and I explained that everyone so far had done it for free. He promptly replied with his "charity" rates but suggested that if I can "get them to pay more, we can share the extra cash". I guess that's the kind of business plan you can write on the back of a beermat.

* * *

On the evening of May 24th 2003, Nadia had disappeared into the bedroom. I realised I hadn't seen her for a while so went to check she was OK. I found her leaning against the window sill.

'I think the baby is coming!' she said.
I called an ambulance and the paramedics agreed the baby was on its way. We had to get to hospital as quickly as possible and Nadia narrowly avoided giving birth in the ambulance.

Aaliyah entered the world at 3.13am and we couldn't have been happier or more proud parents. Those first few weeks were totally magical. Becoming a father made me even more determined to keep out of prison and provide for my precious family. I wanted Aaliyah to have a totally different upbringing to mine.

We were nervous parents and for the first time I started wearing a seat belt. I realised I was responsible for someone else and it weighed heavily on my shoulders. It was obvious we had outgrown the flat, which we had always intended would be a short-term solution. If it had been up to me, we would have moved to Brighton, an area in which I had always felt comfortable. My brother lived in the town and I liked the vibe. I had visited many times as it was the destination for the interFACE crowd to go clubbing before my prison term.

The only problem was that Nadia's family all lived in Pitsea, Essex and with me working obsessively on the business, it was important for Nadia to have the support of her relatives nearby. We gave up the flat in Chadwell Heath and move to a rented house near her family.

* * *

Lee Barclay had recently been released and he got in touch and said we should have a catch up as there were "some developments". I was intrigued. After we had come to the realisation that Stewart Carroll had grassed us up, he'd put the word out on the street that we thought that was the case. If Stewart was innocent, he'd have protested very loudly, if he wasn't, he'd have gone into hiding. Stewart and his family quickly disappeared from London so our suspicions had been confirmed. I suspected this was what Lee wanted to talk about.

We met in The Barge pub in Pitsea. He told me Dylan had just been released too. I knew Dylan had been ill while he was in prison. He'd been diagnosed with skin cancer but had made a full recovery. What I didn't know was that whilst he was inside, he and Amanda had been corresponding and they'd decided they were in love and wanted to give it another go. Amanda thought it best that she was honest with Dylan so told him she'd slept with me, and Dylan's best mate Gerald.

'So?' I said 'She wasn't with him when I slept with her. They'd split up'

'That's not how he sees it' Lee told me.

He then went on to tell me that Dylan had tracked down Gerald and beat him up so badly that he was in intensive care.

'And that was his best mate, so think what he's going to do to you!' said

Lee.

I didn't even want to think about it.

'The thing is, Jacko, Dylan knows you're in my firm and if he goes near you then he'll have me to deal with'

I felt instantly relieved. I always thought Lee and I had got on well inside and that we had a genuine friendship

'So....' said Lee, 'I need you to do a little something for me'

Suddenly it became very clear what Lees game was. I didn't doubt the threat of Dylan was genuine. But Lee's nothing if not a smart operator. And he was seeing how he could use the situation to his advantage.

Lee explained that he was out of the drugs game - "too risky" - and was now involved with Giro fraud. He needed forged driving licenses made and he knew it was something I could produce.

The message was pretty clear, if I didn't do it, then Dylan would be told that I'm fair game. Do as Lee asks and I'll be safe.

I didn't feel like I had much choice so told Lee that I'd do it.

When I got home, Nadia could see I had something on my mind. She'd already been wary about me seeing my "old friends" and now she knew something was up. I've never been able to hide anything from her so I told her all of it.

She didn't even have to say anything. I looked at her face and said 'I'm going to tell him to shove it'.

To this day I still don't know where I got the balls to do what I did next. I left the house and went to a nearby payphone and called Lee. It was an old habit - using payphones to talk to Lee - it was less traceable than using a mobile phone.

'I've changed my mind' I said, 'I'm not doing it.'

'Are you fucking crazy?' Lee shouted 'Do you understand what Dylan will do if he finds out where you live?'

'Do me a favour' I said to Lee, 'Give him my address. I want to get this out of the way sooner rather than later'

And with that, I put the phone down and walked home. I had no idea what would happen next. Would Lee really tell Dylan I was fair game? Would he tell him where I lived? How soon would he come?

The next day my phone rang and then stopped. I saw it was a missed call from Lee. So I went to a different payphone and called him.

'I'm not changing my mind' I said as soon as he answered the phone. 'Never mind that, Jacko. Go and buy a lottery ticket!'

'What?' I asked. I was totally confused now

'You're the luckiest bastard I know' he said 'Dylan dropped down dead out of nowhere last night. Brain tumour apparently'

I could swear that as soon as he said those words, the clouds above Pitsea parted, the sun shone through and the birds started singing.

With the threat lifted from over me, I was able to get back to focusing on my new family and fledgling business.

Chapter Thirteen

GROWING PAINS

One day I got a call from the Trust to tell me about an organisation called LYST - London Youth Support Trust. They needed some "computer work" done at one of their buildings and asked the Prince's Trust if they could recommend someone, so my name had been put forward.

I went along to the address I was given, Mare Street Studios in Hackney, to see what it was all about. I was met by a lady called Rachel Rickards who explained what LYST was all about. It had been set up by Rob Whitmore. Rob had been a regional director for the Princes Trust and felt more needed to be done to support business beyond the initial funding and support. Specifically he saw a problem with the huge leap in costs between working from home and having commercial premises. LYST was set up as a stepping stone to provide subsidised office space.

Their first site in Deptford was now full and they were working on opening this new centre in Hackney. They needed a computer network put in and that was where I came in. It wasn't really my forte but I said I'd get it done for them.

I managed to find someone that could do the job at a good price and sent them in to do it. I went along to see how they were getting on, but I also had an ulterior motive. With a new baby in the flat, it was increasingly impractical to work from home.

Although the rents at Mare Street were already heavily subsidised, it was still out of my reach. So I managed to come to an arrangement with Rachel. Let me have a further reduction and I'll be the live-in technical support for the network. She agreed and I became their first tenant before the centre was even officially open.

I was excited to have my first office - Unit 303, Mare St Studios. Its was a very industrial building but it would serve its purpose. I broke the news to Milton and I told him the space was way too big for just me. He agreed to move in too. It made a lot of sense - the rent would be lower still and we were working with lots of the same clients,

Once moved into the new office, I thought it was about time I did some marketing to find more clients. Actually getting started in business wasn't as difficult as I thought. It really was as easy as finding people who needed what you could offer and agreeing a price. The relationship with Milton worked really well so I thought there must be other web designers out there who needed the same help. The Princes Trust have a "business finder" on their website with thousands of businesses on it. So I quickly wrote a small program that would systematically trawl through all of the listing and give me a spreadsheet containing all of the businesses that offered web design services.

I put together a leaflet advertising my services and Milton worked his magic on it to make it look good.

Out of the 200 leaflets I sent out, I only got one response. Sotiris Spyrou, a Cypriot who ran a search engine optimisation company, trading as the Web Marketing Agency. He asked me to do some programming for him, with which he was very happy. Once he realised how much of his workload I could automate, he found plenty more programming to keep me busy.

He had been established for a couple of years and was working out of a spare office in his brother's company in Southgate. It wasn't ideal and he was desperate to get out from under his brother's wing.

It's a small world, I thought, when I discovered Sotiris and Milton had been to the same college together years earlier. The three of us got on very well and so Sotiris also moved into share the office. We made a great team. I was the programming expert, Milton had the design skills and Sotiris had the expertise in the field of SEO. Between the three of us, there was no web project we couldn't deliver.

* * *

As the work started to build up, so did the paperwork. I'd been using a Microsoft Word template that I'd just fill in each time to create invoices. But it was time consuming and error prone. A number of times I'd accidentally overwrite invoices or send out two with the same invoice number. And keeping track of who had paid was becoming harder too. A nice problem to have, but a problem nonetheless.

I decided to look at what software was available to buy and discovered Sage 50, the market leader in accounting software. With any piece of new software, I had always been able to pick it up and understand it very quickly. But with Sage I found it incredibly difficult to understand and use. I was totally confused by the jargon. It took me a couple of hours of reading through the manual before I was able to create my first invoice. But when it came to the second invoice I couldn't remember what to do and had to go back to the manual.

This was ridiculous - it was taking me longer than it had been before and I didn't really understand what I was doing. I quickly gave up on Sage and tried another product, Quickbooks, which was at best a little bit easier to use but still a long way from being ideal. All I wanted to do was create invoices with sequential numbers and the ability to mark them paid or unpaid. It wasn't rocket science.

But the software wanted to know my "year end" and would talk about a "nominal ledger" and "fixed assets". None of these terms meant anything to me. In the end I gave up and in the course of one evening I hacked together my own solution that did exactly what I wanted it to do. The quickest way for me to program it was on the web, which is exactly what I did. I created a password-protected folder on my website and called it "/accounts". I put all the code in there along with the Microsoft Access Database that stored all of the data. Problem solved, I could now get back on with paid work.

Milton and Sotiris had been through the same pain and asked for a copy of my system. It was easy enough for me to set it up for them so I did.

* * *

The three of us continued to do a lot of joint projects and it wasn't long before we needed an extra pair of hands. So we drafted in my childhood friend Yomi to help out every now and then.

One day, Sotiris and I couldn't agree on who should be paying Yomi for that day. He'd worked on my stuff, on Sotiris' stuff and on our joint projects. We joked that it'd make life easier if we just merged our three companies.

Later that evening, still hard at work, Sotiris and I took a break and went for a smoke out of the window on the staircase. We decided that actually it really would make sense to merge companies. I didn't enjoy the business-y aspects, I preferred to just do the technical stuff. Whereas Sotiris felt he was better at the sales side of things.

By the time we'd finished our second cigarette, we'd come up with a company name: Key One.

The following day we put the idea to Milton, both really hoping he'd be onboard with the merger. But he decided he'd rather stay independent. Although we were both disappointed, we weren't put off. Milton could occasionally be unreliable and would sometimes go AWOL for days. So perhaps it was for the best.

The new company was formed on May 6, 2004, with Sotiris as managing director and I took on the role as technical director. The idea was to carry on what we were doing but to scale up the operation to allow us to hire more people and bring in more work.

We agreed we needed new offices and found a big room in a group of buildings near London Bridge called The Leather Market. It was very plush and twice the size of what we had. It was a whole lot smarter, enabling us to present the right image to clients. LYST helped us negotiate a good deal as the offices were owned by Workspace Group, the same company that provided them with space for their incubators.

Our first new staff member was Dominique Gillespie, Nadia's baby sister. She was just 16 and fresh out of school, I had first seen her when she was still a baby in nappies. She joined as the office junior with the responsibility of sorting out all the paperwork - a task we just didn't have the time to do ourselves. She was incredibly enthusiastic, hard-working and used her initiative brilliantly to get on top of it all. We gave her very little guidance and really threw her in at the deep end. It was perfect timing for us as she was leaving school and needed a job. Importantly, we knew we could trust her.

Dominique tells me she remembers her first day a bit differently. She says we'd given her a huge stack of papers with instructions to "sort it into piles of what's important and what can be binned". HMRC didn't sound very important so she binned everything with that on it!

Our roles were clearly defined. Sotiris would bring in new business and I would build a technical team to look after it all. Sotiris and I continued to attend the Prince's Trust networking group which was still opening up new opportunities. The meetings moved to the offices of DLA Piper, a leading London law firm and they were happy to sponsor the events out of their corporate social responsibility budget.

I was particularly taken by what a speaker had said at one of the events. He talked about the difference between selling a product versus selling a service. It was my light bulb moment, realising that by developing and selling a product rather than selling our time by the hour, we could upscale much quicker.

Sotiris and I brainstormed a few product ideas. I'd created a tool we called "Cloak and Dagger", It was quite technical and not totally above board ethically speaking. It sat in front of a website and when the website received a visit it would work out if it was a human or a search engine. If it worked out it was a search engine then it would show different content - content designed to make you rank highly in the search results for your desired search terms - i.e. "cheap mortgages". It went a step further and served different content to different search engines as we knew the different engines had different ranking algorithms. We ruled out selling that as a product because we realised there was a limited time before the search engines worked out what we were doing and put a stop to it. Also, we thought the market for it - that is the number of people we could possibly sell it to - was probably quite small.

We had a few other ideas of products we could create and sell, but the one that stood head and shoulders above the rest was the invoicing software I'd built. By now, half a dozen of our business acquaintances were using it for free. But I'd had to create copies of it for them as it wasn't designed to be used by more than one person at a time. I knew I could update it so that we only needed one copy from which people could create their own user accounts, but it'd require a fair amount of development work.

I'd built it to work in a web page rather than the more traditional route of something that you download. But I felt that could be an advantage for us. Rather than having multiple versions of the software in use by different people on their own computers there would instead be just the one copy on our own servers. That would make it much easier to deal with support requests and to release upgrades. It also meant we could charge for it on a monthly subscription basis - making it more affordable for small businesses and giving us a recurring income every month. At the time this was pretty unique, but within ten years the whole industry would have moved to this model.

We asked around among all the other small business we knew. They all confirmed what we suspected: Accounting software was too expensive and complicated for them to use, so they were using manual systems or spreadsheets that weren't ideal. There was definitely an opportunity here and we decided we'd go for it.

We just needed a name. We hit on "Spondoolies" but realised none of us knew how it was meant to be spelt. After much more brainstorming, we came up with the name we were going to use "Lollymate".

After another Princes Trust Networking event, a few of us headed to the Red Lion pub in Moorgate. We were excitedly discussing the big new idea with Rachel Rickards from LYST. She thought it was a great idea, but politely suggested we should give the name some more thought. So we went back to the drawing board and came up with the name KashFlow.

Things started happening very quickly. I put in a few days of solid work rebuilding the system so that it would be suitable for multiple companies, all with their own data securely accessible only to them. I created a registration page so that anyone could come along and sign up to create an account. We got a few more businesses using it for free in return for feedback on what features they thought we needed to add to it and how much we should charge.

One of the first things I added was some analysis and reporting. My logic was that as a business owner, you spend all this time entering invoices but what do you get from it other than keeping the tax man happy (and getting paid, of course). It seemed that once the invoice was paid, the data just sat there being useless. So I made it so that you could create a list of "sources" and "sales people" and assign a source and salesperson to each invoice. That way you could see which salesperson brought in the most work, or what sources (website, yellow pages advert, networking event, etc) were most effective.

Our early users said they looked forward to entering their next invoice just to see how it affected the graphs and charts. I knew we were on to a winner.

* * *

But KashFlow wasn't yet generating any money, so I still had to fit in paid work to help cover the costs. It didn't help that Sotiris was struggling to bring in any new work. So I had to go out and bring in new clients as well as do the work.

We felt we needed a cash injection so applied for a bank loan and under the Government's Small Firms Loan Guarantee scheme. We were able to borrow £25,000 from HSBC.

Sotiris wanted to spend most of the money on a major public relations campaign. But I was concerned. It didn't feel like the right thing to do. Rachel suggested we ask the Prince's Trust to try and find someone to give us some advice. The Trust arranged for us to meet with Lindsey Armstrong from Veritas, a big software company. As we drove out to their offices I was doubtful we'd get much attention from Lindsey.. I'd done some research on the company and discovered they were in the middle of a $13bn merger with Symantec, another huge American technology company. As Lindsey was in a very senior role I knew she would have been very involved with it.

So you can imagine our surprise when we were shown into the board room and the entire board of the company were there waiting for us. Incredibly, the board took off an entire afternoon from the deal to give two upstarts the wisdom of their expertise. They were unanimous in their advice: We should not do any PR until we had paying customers and our own successful case studies.

* * *

It was now September 2005. LYST were planning the official opening of their Hackney centre. As someone that had already benefited from the centre, Rachel asked me to say a few words on stage. The idea of having to stand on a stage and speak to an audience was intimidating enough. But then they told me Sir Alan Sugar would be there to whip a tea towel off the commemorative plaque. Also speaking at the event would be Lord Young. I'd never heard of him before so I did a bit of research. He'd been one of Prime Minister Margaret Thatcher's closest allies and served in her cabinet. She'd famously said of him "Other people bring me problems, David brings me solutions."

As if that wasn't impressive enough, I went on to read how he's been

Chairman of Cable & Wireless, President of the Institute of Directors and many other notable achievements in business and politics. A real heavy hitter! He was attending the event in his role as the chairman of the Board of Trustees for LYST.

'I've never met a Lord before' I told Rachel. 'How do I address him?'

'Just call him Lord Young' she said 'He'll probably then tell you to just call him David'

Rachel thought he would be someone useful for me to know beyond just this event, and so she engineered it so that we would have 10 minutes together before going on to the platform. We met in one of the offices away from the mounting hubbub of activity for the main event

'Good to meet you, Lord Young' I said

'Likewise, but please call me David'

I breathed a sigh of relief and relaxed. We chatted about my background and how LYST and The Princes Trust had supported me. After explaining KashFlow, I was able to give him a quick demonstration on a nearby computer. He asked me a few questions and I was surprised by his technical knowledge. Rachel knocked on the door and said we should go through to the main hall as the proceedings were about to start.
'If you ever need investment in this, do let me know' David said as we left the room. I'm sure he was just being polite.

Our speeches followed. I nervously rambled through the story of how LYST had been very useful for me and I was relieved when I could finally get off the stage and tuck into the buffet.

As he was leaving, Lord Young came over and gave me his business card and asked to keep in touch. It was a nice gesture but I didn't think it was any more than that. I had a rule I played by when meeting people that were higher up the business food chain than me: I'd never ask for their card and instead wait to be offered. The way I saw it was that they'd be more likely to be willing to help or respond if they'd offered their card than if I'd asked for it. This was in stark contrast to Milton, who would run around networking events collecting business cards like trophies, which only ever led to unanswered emails.

Rachel grabbed me before I left and said that I really should follow up with Lord Young.

OK, I'll email him' I said.

'Make sure you do!'.

After the event, I did get in touch and we had a couple of meetings. He asked lots of questions about the business and Sotiris was quite wary of him. The two had never met but Sotiris was cynical and convinced the business guru was going to rip us off. After the meetings and a series of emails, Lord Young stopped replying to me.

As much as I didn't want to admit it to myself. I suspected I knew exactly why he'd gone quiet on me. I'd really struggled to explain Sotiris' role in the business or what it is he does. I thought Lord Young had concluded that he was dead wood in the business, but he was a 50% shareholder and a Prince's Trust supported business, so Lord Young felt it wasn't right for him to say anything.

Whether Lord Young thought that or not, it was hard to deny that Sotiris was not bringing much to the party. We were burning through our loan from the bank on just our monthly costs. The office wasn't cheap. Dominique wasn't paid much, but it was still an expense. I needed to take my salary every month and so did Sotiris.

The only new work that was coming in was work I'd created. And I was then the one doing the work. Sotiris was determined to spend all of his time trying to market KashFlow, even though it really wasn't ready for a big marketing push just yet.

When we were short on cash, we'd pay ourselves less. It didn't seem to bother Sotiris. If he did not have the money to pay his mortgage he'd borrow it from his brother. If I didn't get paid, I was screwed. We had different levels of drive and it was beginning to worry me.

The reporting features I'd built into KashFlow showed very clearly that Sotiris was bringing in far less money to the company then he was taking home. So I was having to do enough paid work to pay for everything and fit in KashFlow development too. Sotiris could see it too and I told him I was worried that we were going to run out of money before the end of the year. He told me not to worry, that he had a plan and we would be fine. But when I pushed him on the details, he couldn't give me any.

October 2005 came to an end and our financial situation wasn't looking any better. 'Trust me' Sotiris said.

Chapter Fourteen

A DIVORCE AND A MARRIAGE

Dominique was now aware of our severe financial problems and during one of our train journeys into London she told me she could not understand how Sotiris generated any income. As much as I liked having Sotiris around, it was apparent that we needed to go our separate ways and that I would be better off without him. The problem was, he owned half the company and we owed £25,000 to the bank.

As the end of November approached, the coffers were virtually empty. Sotiris came to the rescue by putting £5,000 from his personal credit card into the business to meet our obligations. I was grateful he did it to keep us afloat but I knew it was only a short-term solution.

I realised that Sotiris really did have a plan, and he was confident in it, but he wouldn't share it with me. Which made me suspect he was kidding himself. The plan was probably no good so he didn't want to subject it to scrutiny as he knew he'd have to admit to himself that it wasn't going to work.

There was only one thing to do. Sotiris and I adjourned to the pub to have a serious conversation about our plight. I had written down a dozen different solutions to our problem and yet I knew only two of them were viable. But I felt I had to let Sotiris talk through the other options and rule them out himself.

The only viable option was to split the business in half with Key One concentrating on web development and KashFlow continuing to develop the application with the intention of making money from the product. We would each take a company but the question was who would take which bit. Sotiris couldn't take Key One because he didn't know web development. He wanted KashFlow because he said he had a plan to market it. But he would need me to program it and after a bit of negotiation we agreed an hourly rate.

All that was left was how to deal with the bank loan and we agreed it was not fair for either one of us to take it on. We knew if we didn't pay it, the bank would take everything, including the KashFlow product and it would never see the light of day.

As Key One would be left with the loan, and I was to keep that business, we agreed it'd make sense for him to pay £12,500 - half of the loan amount - to Key One so that he could take away the KashFlow product as a new business.

It wasn't that I didn't think KashFlow had a future, I still believed in it. But I was so sick of the situation I was in that I was willing to let it go.

All that he needed to do now was to transfer the money. he said he didn't have it to hand but would easily be able to borrow it from his family. With that concluded, we both got horrendously drunk.

* * *

A couple of days later he said he was struggling to get the money together and would need a bit more time. It was early December and Christmas was fast approaching.

I was massively demotivated because until he came up with the money, I couldn't see a future for myself or the business surviving into the New Year. I didn't know where to focus my efforts because I still wasn't sure what - if any - business I would own in the new year.

Eventually Sotiris conceded he couldn't get the money together. Because we each owned exactly 50 per cent of the business we couldn't force each other to make a decision. We could very easily have ended things there with a stalemate. But then Sotiris offered to sign over his shares to me and walk away. He said he felt guilty for getting us in to the situation we were in and thought it was the gentlemanly thing to do.

He asked for only one thing in return. He thought KashFlow had real potential and wanted an agreement that would give him a percentage of the profits from it for a number of years.

I accepted his offer on the spot. To get the agreement drafted I went to DLA Piper, the law firm who supported the Princes Trust networking events. They said they'd do it without any charge. I told Sotiris to make sure he was getting good legal advice before he signed the agreement. He assured me he was. The first draft of the contract was incredibly one-sided in my favour. I was amazed at how lawyers can take a simple verbal agreement and weave a 5 page document from it full of legal jargon. My lawyers told me that if he was prepared to sign on the dotted line, I could take it he wasn't being advised by a professional. Sign he did. And just days before Christmas I took total ownership of the entire business, including KashFlow.

We parted on good terms. It was a huge weight off my shoulders and I wanted to use the Christmas break to recharge my batteries. I knew I had a bloody big job on my hands in the New Year. I was very relieved that it was all sorted and the outcome could not have been better for me. I had every opportunity ahead of me, even though I was burdened with a £25,000 bank loan.

Nadia and I celebrated the New Year. I was tremendously fired up and Dominique and I were ready to take on the world.

* * *

With the Christmas holiday out of the way, I was pleased to be back in the office. There was so much to do and I was excited by the possibilities that 2006 held for us.

We sat at our desks that first day back in the office and Dominique opened the post. There was more of it than we expected. As she opened the letters, one after the other, she looked increasingly concerned.

'You better look at these' she said quietly.

The letters were all bills, many of the Final Demands. Sotiris' master plan had turned out to be nothing more than throwing shed loads of money into advertising but negotiating to not pay anything for 90 days. He had just hoped something would stick and bring in a load of money. Once we unravelled everything we realised that we owed nearly £70,000.

It was a foolhardy plan at best. The stupidity of it speaks for itself. But he had kept it secret. It was incredibly annoying that Sotiris had not discussed it with me because I would certainly not have agreed and we would have come up with a better solution. It was a desperate last-ditch attempt on his behalf.

There were around a dozen companies that we owed money to and he had told them all the same thing 'As soon as money comes in, you are top of the list to get paid'. I decided that I had to take action and Sotiris' way of doing things wasn't going to cut it.
I drew up a list of the creditors - the people we owed money to - and invited them all into the office for back-to-back meetings on the same day.

I played each meeting exactly the same. I explained that I knew they'd been told that they were Number one on the list to pay, and then I showed them the actual list of everyone we owed money to, and their position on the list

'I'm going to pay everyone in this order. It'll take me some time, but I will pay you' I said. 'You can either sue and shut me down and you won't get anything, or you can give me some breathing space and I will do my best to pay you over the next 12 months'.

Amazingly, they all agreed. My transparency and directness had paid off. Or maybe they all just thought it was better than getting nothing. We lived to fight another day. All I had to do now was to do work out how to pay them back and keep ourselves afloat at the same time. So I dropped Lord Young a short email to explain to him that I now owned 100 per cent of the business and that perhaps we could have a discussion if he was interested in investing.

He replied within minutes, proving to me that Sotiris had been the sticking point for him as I had suspected. I arranged to see him that week. I was very open with him about the debts but also that I thought there was a huge opportunity for the KashFlow product. He could see the potential but was not interested in the Key One side of the company. He suggested we formed a new company and he'd inject £100,000 to get it up and running.

I made it clear that I thought just having his name involved with the company would give us a lot of credibility and I intended to make sure the whole world knew he was involved. 'A Lord on the Board!' He laughed and said he was fine with that.

By the beginning of February 2006 we formed KashFlow Software Ltd. He transferred the first £25,000 immediately, although later admitted that it had crossed his mind that once he had given me the first tranche of money, he would never see me again, or might catch me driving past in a flash new car with some new clothes. But there was no fear of that. I was so glad to have his support.

The cash was great because I certainly needed it. But it was his support and his belief and trust that meant so much to me. There was no one else to whom I could have turned, and one of the first things he said to me was that he would always be there for me and I shouldn't hesitate to call on him. Obviously, he wanted to make sure his investment was safe and it wasn't time for a celebration as I knew there was a lot of hard work to do.

I sent Lord Young the papers for him to sign to formally appoint him as Chairman of the company. He replied saying he couldn't officially take the role as he wouldn't be involved in the day-to-day running of the business. I must admit I was a little disappointed as I wouldn't be able to leverage his name as much as I would have liked.

* * *

Whilst the deal with Lord Young was being finalised, a problem cropped up in my personal life.

Joey thought a lot of me and it really annoyed Nancy when her mum would compare her boyfriends to me - usually not in their favour.

I don't know what was going through her head when she did what she did, I suspect she wanted to bring me down a peg or two in her mum's eyes. She said to her 'You wouldn't think Duane was so great if you knew what he did to me when we were younger'. The implication was that I had forced her to sleep with me.

I spoke to Nancy and told her she needed to go to the police if she really thought that was the case. Lucy tried to mediate but to no avail.

I spoke to Joey on the phone about it and promised her it wasn't true. Nancy later retracted her allegation and never did go to the police but the damage had been done. My relationship with Joey, Lucy and Nancy never recovered..Joey died from cancer a few years later but I didn't find out until months after the funeral.

* * *

Dominique and I were still travelling into the office every day from Essex and one day as we were sitting on the train she said 'I know it might be a stupid question, but why are we spending a combined 30 hours each week and thousands of pounds a year commuting to an expensive office in central London when it is just the two of us?' I couldn't think of a decent answer.

Immediately we arrived at the office I handed in our month's notice and spent the day looking online for offices closer to home. It was glaringly obvious the right thing to do and when I ran the plan past Lord Young he had no objection to KashFlow moving out of town.

We found a dirt cheap office near the main roundabout in Pitsea. OK, calling it an office was probably a bit of a stretch. On the roof of the office block were two brick huts. One housed all of the equipment for the Vodafone mast and the other was the new home of KashFlow Software Ltd. But it was all we needed and certainly helped us to save money.

Basildon Echo, the local newspaper wrote up the story of Lord Young investing in my business. The headline read "Thatcher's man aids Pitsea firm". I was annoyed at the way it was written, it made me sound like a star-struck business groupie when I was quoted as saying "He even gave me his mobile number". As a result of that article I became much more media conscious, something that would serve me well in the future.

Our new office was five floors up and then out on to the roof via the fire exit. The office block was home to a mixture of other businesses. We had a back room and a front room.

Dominique and I set up in the front room where we had two desks. I had been working on KashFlow and improving the programme and adding little features. It wasn't long before we made our first sales to people we didn't know, two annual subscriptions totalling £300. Exciting times. It was a major breakthrough in my mind as it proved the model and that people, who we had never met, were willing to pay for it. For me that was really important. I didn't want to charge £600 like other companies did. I wanted to keep it affordable, but that would mean we couldn't afford to have sales people go out and sell it face-to-face to small businesses. The website would have to do the selling for us, and it seemed like it was doing its job.

The feedback from other Princes Trust businesses and our first paying customers were invaluable and guided me on what I needed to add to make it more useful. Two of those companies, Amanda Eatwell's AJE Photography and Barbara Tobias, a fashion designer, still continue to use the software today.

There was no shortage of things that I wanted to do, it was just a question of prioritising.

* * *

Steadily, sales started to come in from direct customers at an annual rate of £150 per account. It wasn't enough to cover all of the bills, so I was still working for Key One clients to make up the shortfall. With the reduced outgoings, and KashFlow having it's own source of funds, I was able to make a big dent in the debts that Key One had and it was almost debt free.

An email came in from a company called Safe Business Services. They said they served contractors and thought our software would be ideal for them. They were interested in buying 160 KashFlow licences if we could do a deal on the price. I was immediately on the phone and we eventually came to an agreement of £100 per licence per year. That was worth £16,000 a year, which was more than I was paying Dominique at the time. But however hard I tried, I just could not close the deal. I realised I needed salespeople to work on bulk license sales.

As well as companies like Safe Business Services, I suspected we could also sell to accountants who had lots of clients. I was comfortable with the technical and marketing stuff but I knew I wasn't that great as a salesman. As much as I was starting to enjoy the marketing side of things - and would go on to become pretty good at it - sales was something I didn't have the people skills or patience for. I was very aware that the best option was to hire someone to do it.

So I started interviewing people for a sales role. We had one girl start and then quit in her first day. Then into the frame walked Paul. Paul was certainly an interesting character. 'I'm a recovering alcoholic' he told us over a pint at lunch time on his second day on the job. The first thing he'd do each morning was call McDonalds to complain about some mythical problem and he wouldn't get off the phone until they'd sent him some vouchers for a free Big Mac Meal.

I told him about the Safe Business Services deal one morning and he just walked out of the office without a word leaving me totally confused.

It was getting close to the end of the day, and Dominique and I had assumed he'd gone for good. It wouldn't have been a major setback, we agreed.

Then in walks Paul, and with him he had a cheque for £16,000 from Safe Business Services. I couldn't believe it. I called them up to thank them for their order, but really I was just checking he hadn't faked it. He hadn't. He really had just closed the deal.

His behaviour got progressively weirder. One day he put his foot on my desk, pointed at it and said "How much?"

"What?" I asked.

"How much do you reckon these shoes were?"

"I've no idea, Paul. How much were they?"

"Go on, guess"

"Err" I looked at the beat up pair of trainers on his feet, not sure what to say "Thirty quid?"

"Two pounds!" he said triumphantly "Boot sale!"

On another occasion he came in in a really bad mood "That fucking bitch! I'm sick of her!"

"Marital problems?" I asked.

"No, my bloody daughter!"

He was talking about his two year old.

He hadn't brought in any new business, but I couldn't get rid of him after he'd managed to close the SBS deal.

Dominique was spending time dealing with emails from KashFlow customers and would shortly be taking maternity leave, so her sister, Teri, came in to help out for a bit.

Teri and Dom noticed that Paul always made sure he left the office after them.

'What happens after we leave?' asked Teri
'Nothing' I told her. 'He hangs about for about 5 minutes then goes'

Then one day he needed to leave early. 'I'm sorry, Duane' he said in ear shot of the others. 'We won't be able to have our daily management meeting tonight'

He really was on a different planet.

* * *

Sales of KashFlow started to pick up a decent pace and I was adding new features to the software almost every day. The beauty of the way the software worked - the fact that it was all powered by a website - meant that any changes were instantly available to all of our customers. There were no upgrades for them to download or different versions for us to worry about.

There was also a downside though. Delivering software over the internet like this just wasn't being done by any other big company. It would later become known as "The Cloud" or "Software-as-a-Service" and be the norm, but back then people were wary of it and that held back our potential growth.

We hired a young guy called Ben to help with supporting customers and we realised we were fast running out of space. I found out that the floor downstairs - actually in the building rather than on the roof - had a spare office so I arranged to view it with the estate agent. It would have done the job, but if we carried on growing it would have soon been too small for us. On the opposite side of the corridor was a huge long office that was also empty. The estate agent told me they were going to have trouble letting it out because of the size of it. I managed to negotiate a deal with him so that we could get the big office for just a fraction more than the other office would have cost and we all moved downstairs.

Paul was driving me crazy. His behaviour was getting increasingly erratic and he was annoying everyone else in the office. He still hadn't brought in any significant deals since closing the SBS deal.

Lord Young suggested it might be a good idea to get another salesperson in to create some competitiveness, so I started interviewing for a new salesperson.

One of the candidates I saw was Michelle Gorsuch. A tell-it-like-it-is, take-no-hostages, northerner. She'd been running her own recruitment business for a number of years since leaving the RAF. She asked about the other people in the company, so naturally I started telling her about Paul. An hour later I realised I was still talking about Paul and my frustrations with him. It had turned into more of a therapy session than a job interview!

I told Michelle I assumed I'd put her off the job.

"Oh no" she said "I can work with anyone!"

I offered her the job and she started the next day. Three days later she came to me and said "He's impossible! It's him or me" It wasn't a hard decision to make. In the short time Michelle had been there, I had heard her on the phone and seen her at work. She had a great way of talking to people and I could see she was a very capable salesperson. Her experience of running her own business made her a really useful person to have around.

So at the end of that day I asked Paul to come in to the meeting room "for a chat". Dominique was off on maternity leave and I didn't want to sack him on my own, so I asked Ben to sit in with me.

As I started explaining to Paul why I didn't see a future for him in the company, his top lip gradually moved further and further up his teeth until it was stuck there. He spent the next 30 minutes with his mouth in this weird snarl. He told me why he thought I was making a mistake letting him go. I just wanted the meeting to be over and for him to leave.

Finally, it was over. We shook hands as he was leaving.

'Actually', he said, turning around in the doorway 'I have some of my business cards in the boot of my car. You should probably come down and get them'

I had visions of him throwing me in the boot and driving away with me

'It's OK, keep them as a souvenir' I said. And with that he was gone.

Years later, I found out from the bosses at Safe Business Services that they had been all set to do the deal with me, and then this weirdo turned up and nearly scuppered the whole thing. Thankfully, despite Paul, they decided to buy on the strength of the product. I wish I'd know that earlier.

Whilst so much of my focus was on the business, Nadia was being a full time mum at home. Aaliyah was going to a local school. Nancy had also moved to the area with her young children and husband. I'd still see her mum, Joey, fairly often. Especially around Christmas time.

Nadia and I married on August 12, 2006, at Hornchurch Registry Office. I didn't have many guests but Ben and his wife came along. Yomi was best man and my sister was a bridesmaid. My brother missed the ceremony but joined us for the reception in the evening. But Nadia had a huge family and it was certainly a day to remember.

I was working flat out building the business, and my beautiful new wife was a full-time mum. We decided to get on the property ladder but to stay around Pitsea near her family. Mortgages were being given out like candy and we got a 105% mortgage on a three-bedroom house. We wanted Aaliyah to have a sibling so we planned to have another baby.

Until this point, Key One was supporting KashFlow and my freelance development work was still bringing in the money. But now came the tipping point, where KashFlow could just about stand on its own two feet. With a bit of prodding from Lord Young, Dominique and I decided to focus purely on KashFlow.

'Don't worry if you can only just pay the bills' said Lord Young. He promised he would help financially if we needed him. It was my safety net, without which I wouldn't have had the confidence to have this change of focus.

On that day we started answering the phones as KashFlow instead of Key One, and changed our email addresses too.

Chapter Fifteen

BILL GATES
AND
MICHAEL JACKSON

I had managed to keep my colourful past under wraps up until now. It was always worrying that it might come out as the potential damage to the business could have been enormous.

There was one embarrassing article in our local newspaper after I met with Microsoft CEO Bill Gates at another event organised by the Prince's Trust in February 2008. The headline screamed 'Billionaire Gates praises ex-jailbird'.

The meeting itself hadn't gone exactly to plan. I was invited to attend a small gathering to meet Bill Gates at the House of Commons. He had agreed a £1 million donation to the Trust, which was to be its single biggest donor gift. There was a lot of excitement in the Commons and money couldn't buy the tickets to attend. Many MPs were desperate to be invited.

It was one of the rare occasions when I was suited and booted. I was quite relaxed but definitely excited at the prospect of meeting him. We were briefed by his people not to ask for photographs as there would only be one opportunity during the event for everyone to get their cameras out.

I gave a talk on how the Prince's Trust had helped me, and Bill Gates responded by saying what a great organisation it was. I then had the opportunity to talk to him on my own and joked that what we were doing at KashFlow in terms of online software was fulfilling a need that Microsoft was not yet able to meet. His response was 'Don't worry, we will soon' and he wished me luck.

I'm not sure what exactly I was expecting of him, but I felt rather underwhelmed by him. He seemed to be on autopilot. I am sure if he had met me 10 minutes later he would not have known who I was or even remembered our conversation.

Within weeks he stepped down from his role at Microsoft and I remember joking that since meeting me, he had seen the future and it made him realise he couldn't compete. What was certainly no laughing matter was that Bill Gates welched on his agreement to donate the million pounds and as far as I am aware never gave a reason for his decision.

So the article in the Basildon Echo wasn't helpful. All it did was to embarrass Nadia at the school gates as other mums picked up a copy and said 'Isn't that your husband?' It was the first time my past had come back to haunt me but at least it wasn't picked up by the national media.

It also came as a complete surprise to Michelle. I'd never told her about it so reading the local paper was the first time she learned about my past. Her husband used to be a prison officer so she had pretty strong views about prisoners. She later told me she briefly thought about quitting but - thankfully for me - decided not to.

* * *

We were growing nicely in terms of customers and I'd added enough features to the software by now that it could compete with the likes of Sage but without the needless complexity and jargon.

Staying involved with The Prince's Trust and being willing to speak to potential donors about my past and how they'd helped me, turned out to be a great way to meet interesting people I'd otherwise never have met. It also meant I got to eat at posh restaurants that I could never have afforded!

In June 2008, I was asked to attend a lunch hosted by the Prince's Trust for a small number of people representing the technology sector who they wanted to impress and get onboard as supporters. I was to give an informal talk and encourage them to put their hands in their pockets.

I made my way to a private dining room at the top of the Gherkin building in the City. It was certainly an impressive location. One of the guests was Michael Jackson, not the singer, but a successful businessman who headed up Elderstreet, a small venture capital fund. Ironically, he had spent 20 years as the chairman of Sage, my biggest rival, and the giant of the industry. The lunch was hosted by Alex van Someren, a successful technology entrepreneur. He thought it'd be interesting to sit me next to Michael as we'd have a lot to talk about.

'Great surname!' said Michael, as he sat down next to me.

We spoke briefly about KashFlow and a few days after the lunch, I had a call from his secretary saying that Michael would like to see me and asked when I was available.

I asked what the meeting was about but she said she didn't know. I explained that I was not going to any meeting without knowing what it was to be about and that if she could find out we would sort out a convenient date. I could tell she was taken aback by my response but said she would get back to me, which she did, explaining that Michael found me interesting and wanted to know more about KashFlow. He wanted to talk further. Whether she knew any more than she was letting on, it was difficult to tell. I agreed to go and see him.

I had read somewhere that the Elderstreet boardroom had a roulette wheel in the middle of it as Michael had also been chairman of the online gambling conglomerate, PartyGaming. It was true. As I sat there waiting for Michael to arrive I was tempted to give it a spin.

As he strode into the boardroom there was no more than 30 seconds of small talk before Michael started interrogating me as to KashFlow's revenue and number of users. He scribbled away as I spoke and less than 10 minutes into the meeting he looked up from his sheet of paper and offered me £1 million for the business. I was surprised but managed to keep my cool and I replied that it was not for sale.

His response was instant 'Of course it is, I have just not offered you enough. How much do you want?' I was shocked by his directness, but I also really appreciated it. There are a lot of people in business that beat around the bush and use a load of unnecessary jargon. Michael certainly wasn't one of them.

I explained that I only owned half the company and as I personally would want one million pounds (it sounded like a nice, round number!) he would have to double his opening offer. He buried his head in his numbers. Then got out his iPhone - which had literally just been released - to do some calculations.

He looked up at me and said 'OK'.

I must have sounded like an echo as I repeated 'OK?'

'OK, two million.' he said.

I told him that if he was serious I would have to talk to Lord Young. I was trying to play it cool but my stomach was doing cartwheels. I was astonished and feeling pretty happy with myself. I realised that if nothing else happened, at least on paper I had suddenly become a millionaire. I was 29 years old and I owned a company for which someone was prepared to pay a lot of money.

I met with Lord Young but his advice was to turn down the offer. He predicted that we could grow the business and that in time I would make a lot more money. But he said that if I really wanted to sell he would support me and get the deal done.

I went for a further meeting with Michael to discuss his proposal. He was about to buy a company that was listed on AIM, the junior stock exchange, called Access Intelligence and his bigger plan was to take over a number of software-as-a-service companies, with KashFlow to be his first acquisition. His intention was that I would work with him on the board. The idea appealed to me as I knew I would learn a lot from him as he had immense business experience.

He asked me to put together some sales projections to take us to the next stage. I did that and then he said he wanted me to pitch KashFlow to some of his investors. Suddenly I had a change of mind. My gut instinct told me that I shouldn't be doing the running. He was changing the balance of power in the negotiations. We'd gone from him trying to buy me, to me having to sell the idea to him and his investors. So again I went back to Lord Young for advice. I said I wasn't comfortable and he agreed that I should not be pitching to anyone.

Lord Young asked me why I was so keen to do the deal. 'Because it puts a million pounds in my pocket' I said. His reaction was calm and he repeated that if we carried on growing the business it would be worth many times that.

I then explained that I had several thousand pounds of personal debts and it would have been nice to have paid these off and have a certain financial security in my life for the first time. It was then that Lord Young offered an alternative to the deal. He said that if I tell Michael I was not interested then he would personally lend me £75,000. There would be no interest and I could pay it back when we eventually did sell the business. I didn't give the offer a second thought. I jumped at it. I told Michael the deal was off and the following day I had £75k in my bank account.

Besides lending me the money, Lord Young had also inadvertently done something else for me. There was no paperwork and no written agreements for the loan. Just transferring me the money like that showed how much he trusted me and how much faith he had in the business. That filled me with confidence.

The money was more than enough to clear my bills and I would have money in my pocket. More importantly, I knew we could take KashFlow to the next level and grow the company even bigger.

But with Michael being the former chairman of Sage, I thought there was some potential publicity to be had. I knew I had to be careful how I went about it though.

I spoke to one of my early customers that I knew well and asked her to post on the UK Business Forums website with the subject line "KashFlow being bought by ex-Sage boss?" She included some links to a media interview where Michael Jackson said he was interested in acquiring online software companies and then said 'Am I right in assuming that Michael Jackson is buying KashFlow? I am not being bothered if he is, I am just being a bit nosy'.

It obviously wasn't a post I could make myself. And having someone else post it had the desired effect. It prompted a whole heap of discussion among the small business community in just a few days and was picked up by some news websites.

When the conversation started to die down I added fuel to the fire by posting a reply saying that I couldn't confirm or deny the rumours. This sparked even more discussion. Finally, I confirmed that we had been talking but the deal was now off the table and I would not be selling KashFlow.

Overall, it resulted in some excellent media coverage as well as lots of new potential customers registering to take a free trial of the software.

I heard via a mutual contact that Michael was furious. I was accused of not being willing to take his money but perfectly happy to use his name for my own ends. I made sure he got the message that I was sorry but thought it the entrepreneurial thing to do and that in time he would have approved, which turned out to be the case.

* * *

On one of my regular catch-up calls with Lord Young, he noted that business was starting to grow very nicely.

'We're in danger of having a real business here!' he said.'It'd probably make sense if we started having proper board meetings'.

I agreed, of course, and we ended the call.

A few minutes later I called him back.

'I'm sorry, David' I said 'I can't have a board meeting with you'

'Why on earth not?' he sounded a bit worried

'Well, do you remember when I sent you the form to appoint you as a Chairman? You never signed them!'

'Send them over - I'll sign now!' he laughed.

And with that Lord Young officially become my chairman.

Chapter Sixteen

THE SAGE WARS

We started to grow quite quickly and soon amassed a couple of thousand monthly subscribers which brought in excellent revenue. Michelle hired two more sales staff and Sandile "Sandi" Dlamini came on board as a developer working alongside me. I had never been academically trained as a programmer like Sandi had.

'Do you have a map of all of the database entities and how they're related?' he asked on his first day. After a quick Google to find out what on earth he was talking about I was able to confirm that no, we definitely didn't have one of those! So Sandi went off and created one and put in place a few processes to make development of new features easier and less likely to break existing features.

On our pricing page we had a table where we compared our prices with those of our rivals, Sage and Quickbooks, and their better-known products. We were cheaper, had better features and I wanted us to shout about it. An in-house solicitor at Sage got in touch saying that the comparison was unfair and that we should change four specific points. Two of them I thought were fair requests so I made the requested changes. I thought we were on solid ground with the other two points, so I refused her request.

* * *

In November, 2008, I was heading to the Business Start Exhibition at Olympia. I took my friend Neil along with me - he had joined to work with Michelle. I couldn't resist first going to the Sage stand to check out what they were doing. Whilst we were offering web-based accounting software, Sage was still only producing traditional desktop products.

I spotted a laptop in the corner of their huge stand and noticed it was running a web-based programme. I hid my name badge and spoke to the two guys standing by the laptop. One introduced himself as Duncan Hawes. They were very proud of what they'd built. They told me it was a new product called SageLive and it was entirely web-based. This was its first public appearance and they hadn't even formally announced it yet.

I asked how it compared to other online accounting software, the first words out of his mouth were 'Like KashFlow?'. I tried to hide my grin and asked if they saw KashFlow as their main competitor for the new product to which Duncan said yes.
I thought it best to come clean so I said 'Good to hear!' and handed over my business card.

There was a ripple effect around the Sage stand as the word went around "That's the KashFlow guy!". I felt like a celebrity.

Once he'd regained his composure Duncan said 'Oh, we're not allowed to talk to you. I'm told there are legal issues between us' I had no idea what he was talking about and he didn't seem to have any other details.

'You know I'm going to have to blog about this, don't you?' I told him. 'You've got to do what you've got to do!' he said. I sensed they were impatient for the Sage marketing machine to start promoting their work and were keen for the world to hear about it.

As Neil drove me back down the A13 to Pitsea, I was in the passenger seat with my laptop out excitedly drafting a blog post about what I'd discovered. The post got a lot of views. although mainly from industry insiders. So whilst it didn't initially do much in terms of getting more customers, it did help to raise our profile within the software industry.

It also meant that once Sage got around to formally announcing the product a few days later, we appeared first in any Google searches for SageLive.

Later that week I got a formal legal letter saying we were being taken to Trading Standards over the outstanding changes Sage had asked for on our pricing page. I immediately realised that this was the "legal issue" Duncan has been referring to.

I'd already learnt that PR is far more valuable than advertising, and this seemed to me to be another opportunity to get some free press coverage. Sage were a global organisation worth in excess of £2 billion and we were a small start-up with a single office on a busy roundabout in Pitsea, Essex. A perfect David and Goliath set-up.

Reporting someone to Trading Standards is somewhat different to suing them. But it was a difference I'd gladly overlook in my quest for media coverage, I used the company blog, my twitter account and all the journalists I could get in touch with to shout about how the big horrible Sage were picking on little ol' KashFlow and threatening to sue us. It worked a charm and we got lots and lots of coverage. Most of it focussed on the angle that we must be doing something right to have provoked such a reaction from an industry giant. It all resulted in more traffic to the website and more customers.

* * *

In early 2009, Nadia and I were relaxing at home. She was five months pregnant and enjoying an episode of EastEnders. Sage had now made their SageLive product available online for people to try so I decided to have a play with it.

It took no time at all to discover three very basic security issues with the programme. From a technical perspective it was very badly built.

The right thing for me to have done would have been to contact them privately and explain there were serious issues with their product. That's the usual etiquette when it comes to discovering security issues. It's meant to avoid the issues being made public and putting users at risk from hackers making use of the vulnerabilities you've discovered. But because of their threat to sue me, the fact they had no users yet and of course, my new-found appetite for free publicity, I decided to write a blog post detailing the security problems.

After detailing the problems, I added a real note of drama by saying "It's at this point I realised that if I went any further then I could possibly fall foul of all sorts of laws about unauthorised access to remote computer systems. I started to worry that the FBI would be knocking on the door any minute"

I sent the link to the world and his wife. It went to every media outlet I could find and the technology press were all over it.

Sage, who were now very wary of me, refused to give any comment. I went on the attack and kept talking to journalists, suggesting Sage had two options. The first was to withdraw the product and admit the security issues or, secondly, they could do nothing and show that they did not care about their customers' data. Either way, I held all the aces.

Soon, a respected computer security analyst from the US took a look and confirmed all of the issues I'd reported and discovered even more. Sage gave in and the product was withdrawn.

Sage announced it as a temporary suspension while improvements were made to the programme. I wrote another blog post to proclaim that "SageLive is dead". The issues were so fundamental and difficult to fix that I knew the product would never see the light of day again. And I was proved right.

But the fun I was having baiting Sage was only just beginning.

* * *

I knew that with the increased profile of the company, I was running a real risk of my background coming to the fore. Rather than leaving it to chance I decided to control how and where it would come out.

Richard Hillgrove, a publicist, helped me plant a story with Martin Waller, who writes the City Diary for The Times.

He published a great piece on 4th March 2009 with the headline: "Sage declares war on KashFlow."

It mentioned the minor detail of them threatening to sue us but also detailed my arrest and conviction. Everyone assumed it was leaked by Sage's publicity machine in retaliation for me causing them to withdraw their new product. I was not about to correct them.

There was a lot of online commentary accusing Sage of plunging to new depths with their alleged smear campaign when my background was irrelevant. I was also relieved to have my background out there in a controlled way. It was a genuine weight off my shoulders. Although I did feel a little guilty about the way I'd done it.

I was in my element in my battle against Sage. I was thoroughly enjoying myself and it was doing wonders for our profile. It was the kind of advertising money just can't buy. I heard that Sage were reaching out to a few people asking them for advice on what to do about me. Richard Holway, the leading UK technology analyst privately advised them that they should buy me out. It made a lot of sense, but it wasn't something they tried to do.

I did feel a bit sorry for them. While they were having board meetings trying to work out how to respond to my most recent strike, I'd already moved on and was attacking them from a new angle.

As Sage are a public company listed on the stock market, there are lots of analysts that write about them. The analysts need to get their heads around new technology to be able to better understand Sages future prospects. So guess who they'd come to to try and figure it out? Yours truly. I'd often spend a few hours with analysts explaining the technology differences and where I thought Sage was going wrong. Of course the analysts wanted to pass these insights off as their own so couldn't credit me. Instead, to repay me for my time, they'd make sure KashFlow got a name-check in their research papers as a great example of what Sage should be trying to emulate. I'm sure this only irritated Sage even further.

* * *

In July 2009, I launched a promotion asking users of Sage to send in their copy of the Sage software along with their receipt in return for a year's free subscription to KashFlow. A good offer that would bring in new customers - we'd make no money from them in the first year but I knew most would go on to pay for the second year and beyond.

What the offer lacked though was an angle that would make it worth the media writing about. But that was easily rectified. I said that once we received enough boxes of Sage software, we'd build a big bonfire with it all.

In the car park behind the office, Neil and I set up a ceremonial burning of one Sage box-set as a teaser. It was really hard to get the box to catch fire and we had to squirt lighter fluid on it. At one point we spotted the police and had to hide. Eventually we got the video shot. We overlaid it with the tune of the Funeral March and posted it on YouTube with the title "The Future of Boxed Software"g r

Once again, a tonne of media coverage resulted and a good number of people sent in their copies of Sage and other desktop products in exchange for our software. We were writing a new piece of software to help people import all of their data from Sage into KashFlow so having lots of different versions of Sage lying around made it easy for us to test it. The last thing I wanted to do was burn the software.

I contacted the local environmental agency and asked what the fine would be for an unauthorised fire in a public space. Their response was very specific: I would be liable for a £25,000 fine.

Perfect! I sent out a press release saying we had to call off the bonfire due to threats of a fine from the local authorities. It gave journalists an excuse to write yet again about our aborted software bonfire.

Sage tried to hit back with a counter offer of a 20 per cent discount to businesses if they sent in their copy of KashFlow. A ridiculous thing to do as there is nothing physical to send in if you're using web-based software. The tech press loved it as it further illustrated that Sage just didn't understand new technology. In fact, it helped us get new customers, people were going to the Sage website and seeing us mentioned - a company they'd never heard of before. So they'd search for us to see what we were all about and instead buy from us.

Our increased profile and the growing trend towards the software-as-a-service business model meant I got a lot of interest from Venture Capitalists on both sides of the Atlantic. I didn't really seriously consider taking money from VCs as something I wanted to do. It would have meant being answerable to them and I didn't want to give up control of my business. I was very much in charge of my future and wasn't going to be at the mercy of someone else's timetable and motives.

I was on the phone with a salesperson who was trying to sell us some advertising and he said 'Now that you're well known...' then he corrected himself and said 'or rather, now that you're known...'. I wasn't listening to the rest of what he had to say because that's when it hit me. Yes, we'd got a lot of media attention, considerably raised our profile and won lots of new customers. But we'd become known as that mouthy company that's always fighting with Sage rather than a company with a good product on its own merits. I decided there and then that'd we'd need to tone it down. A lot.

* * *

While I'd been busy winding up Sage. Nadia had been busy growing a new baby. Sienna-Mae was born on May 9th 2009. It was hard for Nadia, bringing up two young girls whilst I was working obsessively on the business. I'd keep assuring her that it would all be worthwhile and repeated a line I'd heard somewhere "Entrepreneurship is living a few years of your life like most people won't, so that you can spend the rest of your life like most people can't.".

Whilst we weren't struggling financially, I also hadn't yet made any considerable amount of money from the business. With a bigger family we wanted a bigger house - and ideally in a more desirable area. Nadia agreed that a move to Brighton would be a good idea.

I spoke to Lord Young about it. As well as a great source of business advice, he had also proved to be full of wisdom on all aspects of life. He felt it was important that my domestic life was happy and settled as this would mean I wasn't distracted from the business. He suggested I find a nice house - bigger than we actually wanted - and take a pay rise to cover the rent. I could worry about buying somewhere further down the line. It was a great solution and so it came to be. I moved to Brighton with Nadia and our two girls.

Chapter Seventeen

LONDON CALLING

We were starting to gain a decent profile as my appetite and ability for self-publicity grew and helped spread the word about KashFlow. We started to get approached by various potential investors, especially those interested in the technology space. "Software as a Service" or "The Cloud" was the hot new thing and we were at the forefront of it.

Often, potential investors or partners would want to meet in London. Being based where we were in Pitsea meant that if I went into London it would pretty much write off the whole day. So I'd try to make sure that if I was going into town, I'd have a few meetings on the same day to make it more productive. This did mean that I'd miss out on possible opportunities by not going in to London.

William Reeve was one potential investor who stood out from the rest because he took the trouble to meet me in Pitsea rather than insisting I come to London. We arranged to meet at a pub called The Bull. It is an old fashioned proper spit-and-sawdust kind of pub, certainly not the type of city wine bar where he was used to meeting contacts. I spotted him as soon as he arrived because he was the only person in the pub (and probably a few mile radius) wearing a suit. When he ordered a white wine you could have heard a pin drop in the bar. I am not sure the last time they uncorked a Chardonnay but William was totally unfazed, taking it all in his stride, even though he realised he looked totally out of place.

We sat in the beer garden where a fierce-looking pit bull kept coming up and sniffing William's leg while we tried to talk. Despite this four-legged beast hovering around us, we had a relaxed chat and William asked a series of questions that really got me thinking. If I took investment, he asked, what would I do with the money? I explained I wanted to move our offices to London. It'd be closer to the action and would mean we could attract better staff. In particular, there was a guy I wanted to head up the technology side of the business and he wouldn't commute to Essex from where he lived on the south coast.

He suggested I should do my sums and work out exactly how much I would need. He thought I might be surprised at how little it would actually cost. He knew he was talking himself out of an investment opportunity, but he said he thought we might be able to make the move without any investment. At first I was doubtful, but when I did the maths, it did indeed look like I could make it work on the current income. But it would leave the business with no margin for error. One unexpected expense or miscalculation would leave me without the money I needed to pay the rent or the wage bill.

Once again, I turned to Lord Young. He looked over my numbers and agreed that, in theory at least, we could do it without needing further money. But he also agreed it was a very close run thing. He told me I should make the move and if I ended up short on cash then to let him know and he'd loan the business whatever it needed to make up the shortfall.

It gave me the confidence to start looking for new offices in London. Without his backing it would have been too risky. Dominique had no qualms about the move as we had worked together in London before the switch to Pitsea and she felt the time was right to move back. However, Michelle, who was in charge of sales, was not so sure about making the move. She wanted time to think about it. I lined up office for us to view the next day. Michelle knew we were doing the move with or without her. Although I'd certainly prefer that she came.

With staff coming in from Essex, and me (and hopefully, my new CTO) coming in from the south coast, we were limited on where in London would be easily reachable for everyone. Taking Fenchurch street and London Bridge as the two entry points from the east and the south, we worked out that somewhere around Tower Bridge was our best bet.

I called Sanchita Saha who runs Citysocializer.com. I'd met her through the Prince's Trust and had built the first version of her social networking platform. I wanted to ask her if there was space in the building she was based in in London. It turned out she had just been told she'd need to move premises too so I promised I'd keep an eye open for anywhere that looked like it'd work for her and her fast growing team.

It was a long hard slog as Michelle and I went from one office to another. There was one that we thought we could make work, but the others were just no good. Our feet were killing us by the time of our final viewing. We arrived at the office on Tooley St and immediately sank into the chairs they had in the meeting room. There was a company already based on the whole of the first floor, but they had too much space so were willing to divide it into two and rent out half of it. As we sat there moaning about our aching feet we realised that this place was actually perfect. I suspected that Michelle had just had enough of the walking and agreed with me to shut me up. I told the estate agent we'd take it.

It really should have been as easy as agreeing the lease and letting us have the keys. But I was wearing jeans, t-shirt and trainers. The company that were renting it out weren't taking me seriously and did not think for one minute I could afford the rent. They wanted me to give them what's called a Personal Guarantee - this meant that if the company failed to pay the rent, then I would personally be responsible for it. I'd always been advised never to give personal guarantees, so I refused. It was incredibly frustrating. Lord Young suggested I threw his name into the mix and he went against his own advice and offered give a personal guarantee for the first year. His name alone certainly made the landlord start taking me a bit more seriously, but they then asked for us to give them a years rent - £60k - to hold on to once Lord Young's personal guarantee expired after the first year. Having £60k of money tied up doing nothing isn't good business sense, but reluctantly I agreed.

Shortly before signing the lease I had a very odd phone call with the landlord. I could tell he wanted to say or ask something, but just wouldn't come to the point. I'm not very good at reading between the lines. Eventually he said 'The things is, none of us have actually seen Lord Young yet'. I paused. 'Would you normally have to meet him in person? You have his signature on the lease document already'. There was a long silence at the other end of the phone. 'Well, no. I... er. I'm sure it'll be fine'.

It dawned on me that they clearly thought I'd made up Lord Young's involvement. It wasn't the first time I'd noticed that my relatively young age and laid back approach to business had gone against me.

Eventually they agreed and the deal was done. I had a team of eight but the office could easily accommodate 25 people. So I came to an agreement with Sanchita: I sub-letted half of the office to her. It was only to be a short-term arrangement as we were both expecting to grow quickly, but it made sense to help us both keep our costs down.

It didn't dawn on me until after we'd moved in, but the new office was virtually opposite Southwark Crown Court where I had stood trial. Seeing the prison vans pass with their anonymous passengers behind the tinted glass as I went about my day certainly made me reflect upon how different life was now.

* * *

We moved in to the office in early September 2009, the weekend after I moved home to Brighton. With that now all sorted I now needed to hire Tim as my CTO.

I'd kept in touch with Tim since my time at Farplants and on paper he was a perfect business partner for me. He was very good on the technical side of things, was a trained accountant and had an MBA - everything I didn't have. I'd tried to hire him before. But when I could afford to pay him £16k, he was on £20k. By the time I could afford 20k, he was on 25k. He was going up in his current company just as quick as my available cash was. Early on I tried to offer him shares in the business to make up for the lower salary, but he passed on the offer. I could understand why, it wasn't that he didn't believe in the business, but he had a young family to support and wasn't willing to take the risk. Typical accountant! But with the move to London and Lord Young's financial safety net under me, I was able to make him an offer and get him to agree to come and join me.

Sanchita and her six staff joined us there and the offices were a hive of activity. There was a real buzz in the air. Tim joined and was excited at the prospect of taking control of the complete technical operation and expanding the team so that we could develop as a company and bring a professionalism to the development process. As my aspirations for the company grew, I knew my rather haphazard approach to software development just wasn't going to cut it. Tim taking on that responsibility would free me to concentrate on marketing and the commercial side of the business.

You know how some people just click straight away and get on really well? Tim and Dominique did the exact opposite. It was a clash of personalities and they just rubbed each other up the wrong way. I think they both got a kick out of winding the other one up. They had different ways of managing and as hard as I tried I could not get them to work in harmony.

It didn't help that Tim was used to a very different culture. I remember him asking Dominique where she gets pens from. 'I just pick them up at Tescos, it's the cheapest place around for biros'. 'Right' he said, 'I was hoping the company would pay for a refill for my Mount Blanc'. Dominique had always run things on a shoestring budget. She'd had to, we didn't have much money. Whereas Tim was used to an expense account and a fully stocked stationery cupboard to raid.

* * *

One evening I went for a drink to meet a guy called Narinder Sangha - my friend Neil thought it would be a good idea for us to meet. Being based in London now, I could afford to have pretty random meetings without worrying about how it affected my diary. Narinder told me about a company he had worked with called QSG. They provided a facility for you to employ people overseas. 'For example' he said, 'You might want to hire a bunch of developers in India but didn't want all the hassle of setting up a company there, These guys provide you office space and a HR team and help you get set up, and they run the day to day operations'. I'd heard lots of horror stories about people outsourcing their development work to India. It's certainly a lot cheaper than hiring in the UK. You get great guys initially, but then the provider moves them on to new projects with new clients and you get the third-rate guys. But this was different. The people you hired worked for you, and you only. You hired them and fired them. QSG just provided the building and the ongoing HR stuff.

Tim flew out to Pune, 3 hours outside of Mumbai, and interviewed dozens of applicants who wanted to work for us. He took on a team leader, one developer and a software tester - Jayaprakesh (or JP for short), Ismail and Swati. They joined the firm in their own KashFlow branded office and I was excited at the prospect of improving the software even more quickly. They instantly gelled together and after a couple of months I knew we had the right team in place and the right model to forge forward.

QSG helped us get the most out of them by explaining the cultural differences and stressing how important it was to have face-to-face time every 3 months or so - with either some of us going out there, or bringing them over to the UK for week.

I was keen to increase the team with the aim of rewriting all the software and Tim returned for another round of interviews. Disappointingly, he didn't find any candidates who were as strong as our first three employees. I think the problem wasn't so much with the new candidates, but because he'd done such a good job with the first three people, it was hard for others to compare favourably.

Tim decided to move on shortly after that. It was apparent that we wouldn't work well together. He was more comfortable in a corporate environment where the i's and t's were dotted and dashed. My approach to business was anything but that. The constant bickering between him and Dominique hadn't helped matters either. It was a real disappointment. Thankfully his old firm were more than willing to take him back, and in a much more senior role, so he was happy. And he'd done an awesome job for me in terms of putting us on the right track with a great team. All three of the guys out there stayed with me the whole time I was growing the company and we eventually grew the team to 10 people. JP, the team lead, is by far the most conscientious, loyal and professional person I'd ever worked with.

* * *

My team in London was starting to grow quickly as we needed to employ more people to answer customers support questions, and Michelle hired more sales people.

Sanchita's company was also growing in her half of the office. Thankfully she got her business to the point where she needed her own office just as I was at the point where I needed the space she was taking up.

She moved out and we had a big office all to ourselves. Our first year there drew to a close and Lord Young's personal guarantee expired. We were now due to deposit £60k with our Landlord as per the agreement we made when we moved in. But they never did request it from us.

Chapter Eighteen

AN EXACT NUMBER

Meanwhile, in London, Michelle was building her sales team and the business was growing at a phenomenal pace. We had been achieving 100 per cent growth year on year for a few tears which was very pleasing.

But by around 2010, I was getting increasingly frustrated at the difficulty in growing a solid sales team and amazed at the incredible turnover in personnel. Sales people are a weird bunch; just describing some of the characters we had working for us over the years in sales could probably take up a chapter of this book on its own, but I'll spare you the pain.

Dominique had taken over the customer support team and was doing a brilliant job. She has a natural ability to build teams and make them happy and high performing. In contrast, I was getting caught up in people management and just wasn't particularly good at it. I much preferred computers to people! For the first time in my working life I was not enjoying what I was doing. I could see a time coming when I would begin to hate it.

It didn't help that when we moved to Brighton, we moved into a rented house and I'd promised Nadia that it wouldn't be long before we had a pile of cash to buy our own place.

Lord Young's advice was to stick with the business and be patient. He thought we were obviously on to something great. But he had never forced my hand and had always been supportive of whatever I wanted to do. I reminded him of the advice he'd once given me: you sell a business when it's still growing well - leave something for the next man. He said that if I wanted to sell we should go-ahead and do so. He introduced me to Regent, a well-respected mergers and acquisitions firm. I met with Pradip Somaia, one of their partners, and told him that if he could get me £5 million I would be interested in selling.

He went away and did his calculations. They came back with a spreadsheet to illustrate what they thought the company was worth - taking into account our turnover, our growth and other similar types of business that had either been sold or had a value because they were on the stock market. The bottom line was that they thought we were worth £4.92 million. 'That's close enough!'

The problem was that software as a service was still in its infancy. We had actually pioneered it in this country. It was almost impossible to find similar businesses to use as a comparison for valuation. So there were very few comparable business to use as a starting point for working out our valuation.

I fully expected any potential buyer to expect me to stay with the company for a while. I hoped Regent might introduce me to a magical knight in shining armour who would know how to run the business more professionally than I had. I suppose I was experiencing a drop in confidence and thought I was out of my depth.

I prepared a PowerPoint deck which I presented to half a dozen potential buyers. I quickly realised that, with very few exceptions, most of the people I was pitching to were not any better than me at running a business. Although they were from the software industry, some of the questions they were asking showed they just didn't understand this new-fangled way of developing and delivering software over the internet.

I was also losing faith in Pradip. He was one of those people that knew everyone, but no one knew him. In meetings with potential buyers he'd be on his phone and would occasionally chip in with a comment that was not only nonsensical, but was also on a subject we'd moved on from 15 minutes ago.

When I tried to discuss negotiation tactics with him he'd resort to the same joke 'I'll just tell them "The price is ten million, what's your question?"'. If it wasn't funny the first time, it certainly wasn't by the seventeenth time I heard him say it.

One of the people I met in this process was Subrah Iyar who had founded a business called Webex and sold it to Cisco for £3.2 billion in 2007. Subrah was coming to the end of his contract with the giant firm and was looking around for his next venture. It was June, 2010, and after my presentation we went for a coffee. He made it clear from the outset that he was not interested in buying the business outright. He might consider investing but was actually more interested in how he could help me personally.

We spent several more afternoons drinking coffee and talking business as we watched the world go by. Whilst I'd often got praise for getting the business to where it was without any significant cash injection, Subrah made me realise that the real miracle was that I'd got it this far without a senior management team to support me. 'The CEO's job is a great job'. he said 'The reason you're not enjoying it is because you're trying to do four other jobs at the same time'. It was a real eye opener for me. 'Hire the right team, come up with a proper business plan and get everyone working on it. You'll love your job again'. He gave me a renewed impetus which helped me to see a way forward to grow the business.

Ultimately Regent received a few offers but they all came with certain terms and conditions which I couldn't accept and in the end none of them were particularly compelling. With the lack of suitable offers and with Subrah's advice ringing in my ears, I told Pradip I was taking KashFlow off the market and would not be selling.

I spent the next month focusing on the business and was completely re-energised - a fact that reflected on the entire workforce. So I was somewhat surprised when I got a call from Pradip at Regent saying he now had interest from one of the companies he had originally approached and who had only just got back to him.

Exact, he explained, was a large Dutch software company and were keen to meet me. My initial reaction was that they were too late but he persuaded me to meet their CEO Max and their Head of Legal Jeroen. Half-heartedly, I went through my presentation, which by now I could do with my eyes closed.

I reached my final slide which was simply: Any Questions? 'We don't have any' came the response, 'but we still want to buy you'.

I was totally shocked as I had not put any effort into the presentation. I asked how much they would be willing to pay and they asked how much I wanted. It was a stalemate on the valuation as neither of us wanted to be the first to lay down a number. We both knew the rule that whoever moves first loses. I knew what Pradip's response would be, so I didn't want to involve him!

I really wasn't too keen to sell the whole business. I knew it still had a long way to go and I was feeling confident that I could do what needed to be done. But we were still living in a rented house in Brighton and some cash would certainly have come in handy. So I asked if they'd be interested in buying a smaller stake in the business rather than the whole thing. I hoped they would want five or 10 per cent. But Jeroen said without any hesitation that the smallest percentage they would consider was 51 per cent. Because of how quickly he'd said it, I knew they meant it. And to me, selling 51% meant selling control. I'd rather sell 100% than be left with 49% of a business I no longer controlled.

So I told them to let me know what information they needed to be able to give me a valuation for buying the whole business. I told them that I didn't want any distractions, so this wasn't going to be a negotiation - they'd need to make me their best offer and I'd either accept it or decline within 24 hours.

Within a week they put an offer of £6 million on the table. It took me two minutes to tell them that, although I was extremely flattered, it was not in the region of where I wanted it to be. I thanked them very much and said I was sure our paths would cross in the future. I had stuck to my guns and there had been no negotiation.

Nonetheless, I spent the next couple of days half hoping they would come back with an improved offer. I didn't want to be known as the man who turned down £6 million and lived to regret it.

It turned out that they hadn't given me their best price and within a few days they upped the ante and increased their offer substantially to £7.5 million.

I talked to their CEO and agreed we would have a deal at that figure but if they tried to reduce it after closer scrutiny of the business and having done their due diligence I would not be selling. Again, I was relying on the wisdom I'd gained from Lord Young. He'd bought many businesses, especially in his time building up Great Universal Stores. He'd told me the trick was to make a high offer, and once the owner accepts, he already mentally spends the money: a yacht, a super car, etc. So when you later lower the price he's already mentally committed to his new boat and accepts the lower offer. Don't put yourself on the yacht was his advice. I made it clear I would not accept a penny less than £7.5 million.

I also explained to him that I was in the process of changing the way we sold to accountants, which would mean that the money we were making from them would temporarily decrease. We talked it through and he agreed it was a good move and I should continue with it as over time it would be more profitable and help to drive growth.

A team of seven came to look through the business and were holed up in Lord Young's offices for a week. It felt as if they had sliced off the top of my head and were scooping out my brains with a spoon because most of the knowledge of the business was between my ears. They were happy with everything they saw, and they saw everything!

They went ahead and put together the legal document for the sale of the company and we arranged a meeting to confirm everyone was happy ahead of the signing date only weeks away. We were so close, but I wasn't putting myself on the yacht just yet.

I'd hired Rob Carroll, a freelance CFO and spreadsheet wizard, to help with the number crunching involved with the transaction. On the morning of the meeting he called me.

'Hi Rob, don't worry - I wont be late' I assured him. He knew what I was like with early morning starts.

'Have you had a good look at the contract?' he asked. He sounded worried.

'Of course' I said. It was a beefy document and I was really relying on others to interpret a lot of it for me.

'Clause 16 point 9' he said, 'What that effectively means is that they'll be clawing back about two hundred and fifty thousand pounds the day after you sign'

It turned out that there was a clause that had been confusingly worded, but once it was unravelled it meant that because the sales via accountants had declined - exactly as I'd said it would - they'd be reducing how much they paid!

We gathered for the meeting at our office in Tooley Street and as soon as they had sat down I started asking what it was all about. They tried to justify it with flimsy reasoning over the reduction in income. But I quickly pointed out that this was not what I agreed with Max, who by this time was back at his headquarters in The Netherlands.

'You need to get him on the phone and get the clause removed' I demanded. I left the room with my team, allowing them to talk to Max in private. They were in there for about 30 minutes and we could hear heated exchanges - in Dutch.

I may not have understood what I could hear through the walls, but what was clear was the ultimatum they gave me once our meeting resumed. Unless I agreed to the cash-back clause, it was a showstopper. My bum had only just touched back on my chair when I got up again, opened the door and said 'Well, let's stop the show.'

As I showed them the door, I could see the look on Jeroen's face and he was not pleased. He was their chief lawyer and not a man who was used to being turned down. I trusted these guys and as part of my agreement I would have been working with them for two years, which I was looking forward to doing. To me, I felt they had abused my trust, and it was important that both sides stuck to their word.

And that was that. The deal was off. Nadia wasn't pleased. I'd forgotten to tell her not to put herself on the yacht and we'd already made an offer on our dream house. A house we now couldn't afford.

* * *

I was annoyed that I'd wasted months on a deal that never happened. Despite my best efforts, it had become a distraction from running the business. I explained my frustration to Lord Young who, in turn, had been talking to his best friend Nathan "Natie" Kirsh, a well-known property developer and multi-billionaire entrepreneur. Natie had just purchased Tower 42, previously known as The NatWest Tower, for £282.5m. KashFlow was small fry to him.

'Why does he want to sell?' enquired Natie, 'Is there no future in the business?'

'On the contrary' explained Lord Young 'It has great potential but Duane wants to get some cash out'

'Send him in to see me!' said Natie.

The meeting was duly arranged and I explained KashFlow to Natie, and that I wanted to get some cash out of the business to make home life a bit easier. He fully understood, as years earlier he had been in a similar situation and had sold part of his business to raise cash. He said that as a result his new partner went on to make a lot of money at his expense for being a coward.

Natie laughed when I suggested now was the time for him to profit from my cowardice. We agreed a deal there and then based on the £7.5m valuation that Exact had established.

Years back, in the Pitsea office, I'd promised Dominique 2% of the company to make sure she came back from maternity leave. I told her now that she should sell this to Natie that and we'd arrange new shares for her later. So the deal I struck with Natie gave me £1,000,000 and Dominique got a lot of money too. Just as importantly, the business would also get a cash injection to help me hire a senior team.

After months of endless meetings and an aborted multi-page contract, it was incredibly refreshing to agree a deal with someone in less than 30 minutes and back it up with a written agreement that was less than half a page of A4.

It was done - I'd made my first million pounds. Not on paper but real cash in the bank.

I thanked Lord Young for putting me together with Natie. He brushed it off as if it was nothing -

'Let's now concentrate on growing the business.' he said 'No more talk of selling or getting any other investors involved'.

Chapter Nineteen

ALL CHANGE

As we approached Christmas 2011, everything was on track to expand and the whole distraction of getting money in my pocket had disappeared overnight. I had £1 million in the bank and with Naties's cash injection into KashFlow as part of the deal, we were well funded for the future. The New Year was looking like it was going to get off to a great start even before it had begun.

But the old year had not quite finished. A week before Christmas an email dropped into my inbox from Raj Patel, who said he was looking at accounting software in the UK and thought we were an interesting company. He explained a little of his background and that he had been the CEO of Exact for five years.

Hang on. Exact? The same firm that had wasted so much of my time this year already?

I assumed they'd asked him to get in touch to try and resurrect the deal. But it turned out he knew nothing about it. He'd stepped down from the company a couple of years earlier and was only just getting back into the industry. He knew the team there as they'd all previously worked for him, so he contacted them to make sure there was no conflict of interest if he spoke to me. He got the all clear.

We arranged to meet in the bar of the Metropole Hotel in Brighton and drank a lot of whisky. We talked over the industry and then he said he wanted to learn about KashFlow with a view to investing in the business. I immediately liked the guy and found him easy to get on with. He could relate to the struggles I was facing in growing a team.

But I also had to explain my recent deal with Natie, that we didn't need further investment and that my shareholders would not entertain new investors. Raj wasn't put off and suggested he came in for a couple of months for two days a week free of charge to see if he could help out.

All he asked was that after this period we would then look again at any future involvement on his part. Until then there would be no commitment on either side. I liked his honesty and I thought he could be useful. More importantly, I had nothing to lose as he was prepared to offer his help and advice for free.

I was conscious, however, that Michelle and Dominique had been through a lot in the last year and it was important for me that I had their buy-in to Raj getting involved. I made it clear to him that he would have to win them over. I arranged for him to meet up with Dominique and Michelle. I also asked Patrick, a newer employee that I held in high regard to meet him. I agreed I'd let the three of them meet him without me so that I didn't steer the conversation in any specific direction.

The meeting took place over coffee near the office and I waited impatiently for them to return with their verdict. Close to two hours had passed and they still weren't back. I was just about to go and see what was causing the delay when they returned. I didn't need to ask Dominique what she thought - I could see from her face that she liked him. Patrick's verdict was short and sweet: "Awesome". Michelle agreed. They were all very enthusiastic and wanted Raj on board.

Over the next couple of months, Raj fully immersed himself into the world of KashFlow. He helped us focus on better planning and improving our internal communications. One of the first things he did was to get me to call together my management team. I had 20 staff by now and hadn't really thought about who I'd class as being part of a "management team".

After a bit of thought, I came up with 6 names to make up the team.

The first thing that became apparent when we sat down was that the 6 of them had never all sat in a meeting together before. Some of them hardly knew each other! It was evident that because the company had grown organically we didn't have a proper management structure. There were no regular meetings or agreed reporting structures and that was one of the first things we put in place.

Raj headed up the meeting and everyone was very engaged with the discussions. 'Things are going to change a lot over the next few months' he announced 'I'm predicting half of you won't be here in 6 months'

There were shocked faces around the table. I knew this was coming though.

'It won't be because you're fired' he reassured them 'But because it'll be a different working environment - more structured, more demanding - and you might decide it's not for you'

The first resignation came the following the morning. I'd brought in Ben Southworth a few months previously to manage our marketing activities. He explained that he knew what was coming - he'd been through it before building up Jagex, a large games studio. Although he'd enjoyed it then, he didn't feel he had the energy to do it again.

* * *

Within two months, half of the six had moved on. But those that remained, and the hires we'd made since, were much more focussed on growing their parts of the business. With others now taking a share of the responsibility I felt like I was under a lot less pressure. I was learning a lot from Raj and was keen to keep him around. But I didn't feel I could yet go to Lord Young and Natie and suggest him as a new shareholder. So we came to an agreement whereby I would pay him a monthly fee and we would revisit the issue of shares later on.

One of the things Raj insisted I do was a monthly "CEO Update". It involved getting the entire company into a room once a month and I'd give them an update on our progress over the past month. It was then followed by an open Q&A. Because I was always direct and to the point, my team were too. So there was nowhere to hide in these meetings - I was held to account and so were the other managers. It kept us all on our toes and focussed on delivering what we'd promised - whether that be a marketing project, a big new feature or sales numbers.

Michelle was still with us but was struggling to hit her targets. I knew she was not going to enjoy the new way of working and that it was not going to work for her. But I was very conscious of her contribution to our success so far. I was putting off having a conversation about her lack of future with us. But thankfully she saw it too and came to me to say it was time for her to move on. Michelle leaving was the end of one era and the beginning of another.

* * *

The rent on our office was due for a review in a few months time. We thought it made sense to find out what the market rate was for similar offices so that we'd know what a fair increase might be.

We quickly discovered an office around the corner on Bermondsey St. We weren't really looking to move, but Raj just can't resist negotiating a deal.

It was bigger than the office we were currently in. The landlord said he wanted to redecorate and the floor needed replacing. He said he was going to spend £20k getting it all done.

Raj was convinced it wouldn't cost that much, so he convinced the landlord to reduce the rent if we undertook the work ourselves. He got the price down to the same as we were currently paying - around £60k a year.

As if that wasn't enough, he somehow got the landlord to give us the first six months for free.

I found out that the previous tenant was Huddle.com, another London-based tech start-up that had gone on to great things. I took that as a good omen and we agreed to take the office.

Dominique and one of her team, Adam, took on the task of redecorating it. We'd inherited a mish-mash of different desks over the years so decided we'd freshen everything up and get new furniture for the new office. Dominique also arranged for a huge mural to be painted on one of the walls with our logo in it.

The office looked amazing when we moved in. It was a place we could be proud of.

* * *

By now we had competition in the market place. Other companies had seen the potential of online accounting software and released their own products. Our two main competitors were Xero, a New-Zealand based company and FreeAgent, a startup from Edinburgh.

I'd met Hamish, one of the Xero founders a few times when he was in the UK. And I'd often see the guys from FreeAgent around. There were the annual Software Satisfaction Awards - a black tie event - where we'd all be every year and get drunk. Usually after KashFlow won the main award of course! One year 10 of my team ended up at a Karaoke bar with a group from FreeAgent.

When I look at other industries and companies, they see, to keep a distance from their competitors. That wasn't the case in our industry. Perhaps it was the sense of a shared enemy in Sage and Intuit. Or a shared purpose in evangelising about online software.

* * *

I'd continued to maintain a relationship with the Prince's Trust. As the business grew and KashFlow became more widely known I was a good example for them to hold up of the work that they do.

One day I took a call from the Trust and they asked me if I was able to attend an event the following day where they were announcing a major donation. They were unusually cagey about telling me who the mystery donor was, but I said I'd go along and stand on stage alongside the donor and tell my story.

That night at home Nadia and I tried to work out who it could possibly be based on the few clues I'd managed to extract over the phone. We convinced ourselves it would be Prince William.

On the news the following morning we heard that Prince William had just received his inheritance from his mother, Princess Diana. That confirmed it for me - it must be him. I'd met Prince Charles a couple of times at different events, but never Prince William. So I put on a suit and tie for the occasion and headed into London.

When I got to Prince's Trust HQ I quickly discovered I couldn't be more wrong. It was a William, but a different one: the pop star will.i.am.

He gave a great talk about how he'd made £500k from the first series of The Voice and decided not to buy "yet another car" with it, and instead was donating it to the Prince Trust. I then stood and told my story from prison to successful entrepreneur. All the media photos of the day show me standing uncomfortably stiff in a suit with one of the biggest ghetto superstars of the decade.

After doing a few media interviews, will.i.am came and sat and talked with me and a couple of other beneficiaries of the Trust. He said he was blown away by my story and wanted to tell everyone where he grew up about it to demonstrate what you can achieve if you put your mind to it.

Unlike Bill Gates, I found him really genuine and engaging.

A few months later Wired magazine got in touch. They said will.i.am was guest editing an issue and he'd insisted they profile me. I was very proud of my article in Wired magazine, complete with heavily photo-shopped head shot.

From then on, whenever one of his songs came on the radio in the office someone would say "Duane - it's your mate will!".

* * *

I'd always dismissed mission statements, values and company visions as fluffy stuff not worth spending time one. And perhaps that was the right view to have for getting the company to where it now was. But Raj convinced me that going forward these are things we'd need to embrace, as well as a lot of business planning. And he was right.

We spent a very intensive weekend away as a management team finalising the business plan we'd been working on over the past few weeks. It was full of very specific targets and actions that'd we'd be taking over the coming year. Although it was an exhausting period, I almost immediately started seeing the benefit from it.

Because we'd all put a lot of work into the planning it meant that on a day-to-day and week-to-week basis each member of the management team knew exactly what they had to do. They became more autonomous and did not need to keep running to me to make decisions for them. Everyone understood how what they were doing related to other parts of the business and there was a real sense of shared purpose.

We'd presented the plan back to the rest of the staff and answered all of their questions. I was pleased there were so many questions from all levels of seniority because it demonstrated how engaged they all were.

The buzz in the office was almost palpable. We were going places.

Chapter Twenty

AN OFFER I COULDN'T REFUSE

Potential acquirers rarely get in touch and say "Hey, we might be interested in buying your business. Let's talk". It's usually a bit more subtle than that.

So when, in early 2013, I received an email from the Business Development Director at Intuit saying it would be "interesting to explore ways of working together" I knew there was more to it than that.

Intuit are the makers of the well-known Quickbooks product. They are a huge American company valued at more than $20 billion - by far the largest accounting software company in the US for small businesses.. They'd released an online version of their software but it didn't seem to be doing too well. It certainly wasn't slowing down our growth in the UK. We were fast approaching 20,000 customers and our annual revenues was well in to the millions.

I agreed to meet with a group of senior people from Intuit who flew in from San Francisco. My suspicions were confirmed - they were potentially interested in acquiring us. There were holes in their UK operation that they thought they might be able to fill by buying us. We'd just kicked off a huge redevelopment of our software using new technologies and it transpired they were going down a very similar route themselves already. Their new product looked impressive, but it was very similar to our approach so a combined company would have two duplicate products which isn't attractive.

It was a shame that there wasn't going to be any mileage in working with them - they were a great bunch of people and I would have enjoyed working with them. But instead we just drank a load of cocktails at a bar near the office.

* * *

Another potential acquirer got in touch. This time it was one of the largest software companies for UK accountants, IRIS.

Raj and I met with Phill Robinson, their CEO, to discuss ways we could work together. It was immediately obvious that a deal would make sense. They had primarily focussed on selling software to accountants and had built a very dominant position in the UK with relationships with over half of the accountants in the country. Accountants were becoming an increasingly important way for us to get to small businesses and we had a growing number of SME customers and a product that made accountants lives easier. Combining the two companies made a lot of sense with the potential to create a market leader very quickly.

But it was too early to sell. The structure and processes that I'd been putting in place with Raj were only just starting to pay off. We were in a great position to grow the business from strength to strength. Having got a large amount of cash personally also made it a lot easier to say "no" to any potential acquirer.

Raj agreed with me but suggested it'd be a good idea to encourage them to make a formal offer in writing regardless of whether we wanted to take it or not.

"Why?" I asked. I didn't see the sense in that.

"Two reasons," he explained. "Firstly it will establish a valuation for the company and that'll be useful later on if we want to raise money"

"And the second reason?" I enquired.

"It's nice to have a letter like that. You'll just keep it in the draw and every now and then you'll look at it and smile!"

So we told Phill that, whilst we weren't eager to sell, he should make his best offer and we'd give it some consideration. Phill promised to get us a Term Sheet - a letter giving us the intended deal and valuation - by the following week.

* * *

Shortly before the conversations with Iris, I'd given an interview to Duncan Robinson at the Financial Times. They'd written about KashFlow a few times before and being mentioned in such a well-respected paper had helped rehabilitate our image after the Sage Wars.

In the interview my background in prison wasn't discussed. But the article was published whilst I was waiting for Phill to get back to me and it opened with the paragraph:

"On a trip to the US as a teenager, Duane Jackson, the chief executive of KashFlow, had a run-in with the police. Trouble can find a 19-year-old abroad rather easily – especially when he is carrying 6,500 tablets of ecstasy."

It didn't really faze me. My background was already out there for all to see and journalists would often cite it to add a 'human interest' element to their stories. I suspect if it wasn't for my dodgy past then we wouldn't have got half the coverage we'd achieved over the past few years.

In the interview I was asked what I thought about the fact that UK companies tend to sell out before getting big whereas US companies grow in to giants. My answer was the final paragraph in the article and it read:

"It's the genes," says Mr Jackson. "The pioneers, the empire builders, buggered off to America 200 years ago and took all those genes with them. It's the culture over there – they want to be billionaires. Over here it's: '£50m? That'll do.'"

Phill got in touch the day it was published to tell me that the article had scuppered any chance of a deal. I was shocked, I didn't understand why. He explained that his shareholders - a private equity company called Hg Capital - were alarmed that I was "wearing my past on my sleeve like a badge of honour" and that the final paragraph was obviously me trying to create a competitive situation - encouraging others to bid to buy KashFlow therefore driving up the price.

I wasn't at all happy with that explanation. Overlooking the fact that you don't wear badges on your sleeve, my past had been public for a long time - but I hadn't mentioned it in the interview. I could see what he meant about the final paragraph. Others had seen the article and got in touch saying it looked like a perfect "For Sale" advert, complete with the asking price: £50m. But the interview was given before my discussion with IRIS, plus I wasn't the one that wrote the article! Surely he knew how the media worked?

Phill was adamant. No deal.

* * *

I was pretty pissed of about the IRIS situation. It was the first time that my past had caused any major problems for me in business. But I wasn't that interested in selling anyway and we had a great business and a foundation to build from.

Raj and I had become very close through the time we'd worked together. He could sense I was annoyed with the situation and he thought I'd been treated very unfairly.

So a few months later, once the dust had settled, he took it upon himself to make sure I got that letter to put in my top drawer. He knew the guys at Hg Capital, IRIS' owners, and suggested they'd acted hastily and should maybe reconsider and take another look at us.

Shortly after, Phill got in touch with Raj and suggested they have dinner to "catch up". Raj asked me what I thought.

I wanted them to know I was pissed off, so told Raj he should take the dinner but tell them that he was there against my wishes. That way we could start to resume negotiations with them but we'd be in a good position as they'd know they would need to work hard to win me over.

It turned out to be a good move. With Raj there informally instead of me, it was easier for them to have an open conversation. I guess when the founder of a company is in the room you feel you have to be more tactful.

Phill indicated to Raj that they'd be willing to pay a figure that was more than twice what we would have happily accepted a year ago. It was an exceptionally good valuation. But Raj promptly told them it wouldn't do. He said the number would have to be much bigger for me to even bother Lord Young with it given my commitment to not sell the company any time soon after the deal with Natie.

It wasn't entirely true. I'd been keeping Lord Young up to speed on all that was going on. But I'd often use the "My chairman would shoot me!" line in negotiations and it always worked well. The other side of the table can't argue with a man who isn't in the room.

Raj and I spent a week or so wondering if we'd been too greedy and scared them off. But we weren't too worried. We were growing at a very good rate and the industry was maturing quickly and valuations going up all of the time. We could also see how acquiring us made a lot of strategic sense for IRIS and Hg. We were right not to worry. Phill soon got back in touch with a revised offer and put it in writing for us.

When we'd started the negotiations with them the intention was just to get a formal offer - we really didn't expect to want to accept it. But it was a significant amount of money and it was very tempting.

Raj, Dominique and I debated it endlessly. I felt that the competition was about to get a lot stronger - I'd seen a preview of the product Intuit were due to release. To my mind, we could have carried on growing the company for a few more years and ultimately the amount we could have sold the company for then could be less than what IRIS were willing to pay today.

Raj really thought we should reject the offer and go it alone for a few more years.

Dominique was undecided. She agreed we'd both worked so hard for so long and were quite tired now. Then she took a short holiday and came back recharged insisting I shouldn't take the deal.

Lord Young agreed with my views, but he was sceptical that the deal would get done. He couldn't understand why they were willing to pay such a handsome price. But being closer to the industry, I could see why it made sense for them.

Raj and Dominique made it clear that although - if it were up to them - they'd not do the deal, if I decided we should do it then I'd have their complete support.

I talked it over with Nadia. As she wasn't involved with the business day-to-day and knew me better than anyone else, I knew I could rely on her for an objective point of view. Aaliyah was 10 years old now and Sienna was aged 4. I'd missed a lot of them growing up due to my focus on the business. Nadia hadn't had much attention from me either. Selling the business meant I would be able to spend much more time with them.

When I thought about it in those terms, it was a no-brainer. I decided to get the deal done.

Chapter Twenty-One

DOING THE DEAL

It would be nice if, once you'd agreed to sell your company, someone would just write the cheque and the deal is done. But just like my £4,000 from the Prince's Trust, I'd have to jump through some hoops to get the deal done.

The acquirer will want to do their Due Diligence to check everything is what they expect. I'd been through this before with Exact and it was pretty quick if not painless. I was keen to make sure that it was just ask quick with IRIS. If they are going to find a reason to not do the deal, I'd rather it happened as soon as possible.

Phill, Raj and I went out for dinner to celebrate our agreement and to work out the steps needed to get the deal signed.

We ate at Simpsons in The Strand, one of London's oldest traditional restaurants.

"I assume you're not expecting to spend 60 days or anything like that on Due Diligence, are you?" Raj asked Phill.

"Oh no, definitely not" said Phill.

"Great!" said Raj, and tucked in to his steak.

"Hang on" I said. I'd spotted something. "I think we might have some confusion here. Raj - I think that you think Phill is saying it'll be less than 60 days - right?"

"Right" said Raj through a mouthful of food, looking at me quizzically.

Phill looked surprised "I meant there's definitely no way we could get in done in under 60 days!" said Phill.

Raj almost spat his steak out over the table. After getting Phill to repeat himself we both just sat there. We were a little shocked.

"I think I need some fresh air" I said.

"I need a cigarette!" said Raj.

We both got up and walked out of the room. I think we'd managed to make it clear that we were concerned about this new information.

When we went back in, we all eventually agreed to limit the amount of time for Due Diligence to no more than 60 days.

* * *

I'd always been very open and honest with my team about everything. But I wasn't able to tell them about the potential sale to IRIS. Besides the confidentiality I owed them, it would have been too big a distraction for them and would have raised too many questions I couldn't answer.

But all of a sudden there were going to be a lot of people in suits around the office and I'd be spending much more time in meetings than I normally would. So that I had a cover story I told my staff that we were raising a round of investment from Hg Capital. I felt really bad that I was misleading them, but I had little choice.

Often when a big company buys a smaller one, the CEO of the smaller company is asked to stay on for a period of time. Often a lot of his money would be dependent on the performance of the business in the period after the acquisition. This is called an "earn out". I'd always insisted that I wouldn't take an earn-out clause. All of the money would need to be paid in full. Again, this was with Lord Young's advice ringing in my ears. He'd always said to assume you'll never get any money that depends on the earn out and just look at the up-front cash.

Phill agreed and also sensibly agreed with me that I probably wouldn't fit in to the new organisation. It's very difficult to go from being the boss to working for somebody. So we agreed I'd hang around for six months to make sure everything is handed over and then I'd be free.

* * *

Whilst the Due Diligence took far longer than it had with Exact, it was also far less painful. It helped that Raj was leading it so he was the one feeling the pain. Again it was really useful having him lead negotiations over the finer points rather than me. There were a number of points that cropped up that I would have kicked up a fuss over as I was too close to it all. But Raj calmly dealt with it all for me.

With Due Diligence out of the way, we were all set to sign the paperwork to make it official. I was being warned that the process would take the best part of a day. I couldn't see why though.

It was only when I arrived at the offices of the city law firm, Linklaters, who represented Hg Capital, that I realised it was going to take longer than I expected.

I was shown into a boardroom to be confronted by pile upon pile of paperwork. There was a mountain of documents that the lawyers had to go through and dozens of pages that both Lord Young and I had to sign. Thankfully, Lord Young was by my side and he stayed well in to the evening until every document was signed.

At one point we had to hold a ad-hoc board meeting to agree some legal point. This required Dominique's presence but she was at home in Essex waiting for me to phone to say the deal was done. Eventually the lawyers all agreed that she could attend the board meeting by being on the phone and just saying "Yes" to everything. Thankfully that was all she had to do because by the time I got hold of her she was on her third bottle of Chardonnay.

By 10pm the final document was ready to be signed. Lord Young and I sat side-by-side and signed it at the same time.

My journey was over.

In a little over ten years – almost exactly 4,000 days - I'd gone from being released from prison, with a baby on the way, no chance of getting a job and very little prospects to a position where I had millions of pounds in the bank and could provide a secure future for my family.

I hope that by reading this book you've found out the secret of how to do this. The secret is that there is no secret. There was no overnight success or magic button to press. It was a case of being determined, working hard and not allowing yourself to be at the mercy of fate or other peoples will.

There were many people along the way that have been vital to my success. But your own Lord Young and your own Raj are out there waiting to help you when you need them.

Go and get started on building your own future.

Twitter: @duanejackson // #4kdays
Facebook: facebook.com/4kdays

Made in the USA
Charleston, SC
11 January 2016